URBAN VOICES

VOLUME 50

Sun Tracks

An American Indian
Literary Series

The Bay Area American Indian Community

COMMUNITY HISTORY PROJECT,

INTERTRIBAL FRIENDSHIP HOUSE,

OAKLAND, CALIFORNIA

EDITORIAL COMMITTEE

Susan Lobo, Coordinating Editor

Sharon Mitchell Bennett

Charlene Betsillie

Joyce Keoke

Geraldine Martinez Lira

Marilyn LaPlante St. Germaine

THE UNIVERSITY OF ARIZONA PRESS

Tucson

The University of Arizona Press
© 2002 Intertribal Friendship House
First Printing
All rights reserved

This book is printed on acid-free, archival-quality paper.
Manufactured in the United States of America

07   06   05   04   03   02   6   5   4   3   2   1

Library of Congress Cataloging-in-Publication Data

Intertribal Friendship House (Oakland, Calif.) Community History Project.
   Urban voices : the Bay Area American Indian community / Community History
Project, Intertribal Friendship House, Oakland, California ; editorial committee,
Susan Lobo, coordinating editor . . . [et al.].
   p. cm.— (Sun tracks : an American Indian literary series ; v. 50)
Includes bibliographical references.
ISBN 0-8165-1316-3 (pbk. : alk. paper)
I. Lobo, Susan. II. Title. III. Sun tracks ; v. 50.
PS501 .S85 vol 50
[E78.C2]
810.8'0054 s—dc21
[979.4/6004
             2002002848

British Library Cataloguing-in-Publication Data
A catalogue record for this book is available from the British Library.

Frontispiece: "500 Years," © Paul Owns the Sabre

To Joyce Keoke

White Flower Woman (Wahchaska Win)

And to all others who have contributed

to Intertribal Friendship House and the

Bay Area American Indian community

and who are now in the Spirit world

CONTENTS

PART 3 BUILDING COMMUNITY

ILLUSTRATIONS

PHOTOGRAPHS

FOREWORD

Wilma Mankiller

This wonderful collection of essays, photographs, stories, and art chronicles some of the events, people, and places that played a role in the lives of Native families who went to the Bay Area as part of the Bureau of Indian Affairs Relocation Program. When my family arrived in San Francisco in 1957, the people at the original San Francisco Indian Center helped us adjust to urban living. Many years later I moved to Oakland, and the Intertribal Friendship House (IFH) became my sanctuary during a tumultuous time in my life. The IFH was more than an organization. It was the heart of a vibrant tribal community. When we returned to our Oklahoma homelands twenty years later, we took incredible memories of the many people in the Bay Area who helped shape our values and beliefs, some of whom are included in this book.

Justine Buckskin was a one-woman social justice movement for the Bay Area Native community. She was a consummate volunteer, serving on every board remotely connected to the community, and she was the most relentlessly positive woman I have ever met. It was Justine who encouraged me and many others to go to college, including Marilyn St. Germaine. Justine and her circle of friends—including Lou Trudell, Rosalie Willie, Theresa Ballenger, Linda Aronaydo, and Maxine and Susie Steele—were very engaged in the community. They were often joined by Gloria and Glenn Allison, Al Chalepah, Sonny Aronaydo, John Sixkiller, Vernon and Millie Ketcheshawno, Horace Spencer, and many others mentioned in this book.

Then there was Bill Wahpepah, who always led with his heart. Bill was as comfortable working with a street kid battling a substance abuse problem as he was speaking at a European forum on international Native rights issues. Though the original founding documents of the Survival School list a number of us as cofounders, it was Bill who provided the vision and the leadership. He used his awesome powers of persuasion to get people to focus on supporting children and youth. I often wonder what happened to the children and youth who were involved in the school. My prayer is that all the young spirits to whom Bill devoted his life are doing fine.

The Wednesday Night Dinner at the Friendship House was a must if someone wanted to know what was happening among Native people, locally, nationally, or internationally. It was a warm, friendly place where people gained sustenance and support from one another, and it was a place of learning. One Wednesday night there might be a shawl-making demonstration after dinner. Another night, there might be a speaker from the American Indian Movement. Though people often had vastly different political views, they greeted each other in a good way at the Wednesday night dinners.

When the occupation of Alcatraz ended in 1971, a number of people who had been involved settled in East Oakland. They brought with them idealism, humor, a sense of community, and an abiding belief that anything was possible. And indeed it was. At the start of the new millennium, the IFH continues to serve as a gathering place for newcomers as well as the descendants of families who came to the Bay Area in search of the better life promised by the Bureau of Indian Affairs.

The Bay Area Native community and the IFH, like tribal communities everywhere, have had their share of ups and downs, but life is like that. Despite everything, the Friendship House and the community surrounding it face the future with faith, hope, and a sincere honoring of all those who have passed through its welcoming doors.

FOREWORD

Simon Ortiz

"California! Let us go!"

Kaalrrahuul-rree-neeyaa-tsee!
Kaalrrahuul-rree-neeyaa-tsee!
Kaalrrahuul-rree-neeyaa-tsee!
Kaalrrahuul-rree-neeyaa-tsee!

Kaalrrahuul-rree-neeyaa-tsee!
Kaalrrahuul-rree-neeyah-tsee-ee!
Shteh-eh-yuu-uuh!

That's a song my beloved late mother sang a number of years ago when she was telling about the time quite a while back—probably around 1910 or 1911—when Acoma men and boys were going to California to look for work. It was a hard time then, very hard; the people didn't have much of anything, she said, and the beloved men and boys had to leave Aacqu to look for work so their families could be provided for. So that's what the song says: "California! Let us go!"

For many years, people from my Acoma homeland have known California as a place to go to look for work. Like Okies who in the Dust Bowl era of the 1930s and 1940s migrated to California because of drought and dire economic conditions? No, not exactly those reasons. But the economic problems for some Acoma people were owing to difficulties caused by the railroad laying steel tracks right through our homeland. Traditionally farmers of corn, beans, squash, and other crops, Acoma people were no longer able to make a sufficient living after the railroad went through river bottomlands, their best lands for farming, so they had to seek other forms of livelihood, some leaving the reservation, some heading for California.

And then in World War II, young men and women went to California for U.S. military training, usually Fort Ord and Camp Pendleton, and then they were shipped out from California seaports in San Diego or Oakland. I recall myself as a boy waving to "soldier boys" on troop trains headed west, passing through the Acoma reservation. And, of course, numbers of our own service women and men home on leave in uniform were seen at tribal ceremonial activities, social events, and church services.

When our military servicepeople came home, their stories of the Philippines, Guadacanal, Iwo Jima—and later of Korea when U.S. military action took place there in the early 1950s—abounded. A few men from Acoma and Laguna were even taken prisoner by the Japanese army and endured the Bataan Death March. So there were stories of a world beyond the res-

ervation back home, and that world always seemed to feature California prominently because it was a place you went to on the way to a destination—or it was the destination itself!

Needless to say, mentions of California were always rich with stories. Or was it that stories were enriched with mentions of California? Both, actually, especially after the federal
Relocation Program was established and implemented in the 1950s. What was "relocation"
called officially anyway? "Employment assistance" or something like that, I think. To Native American people, it was simply removal and relocation from Native rural homelands
to urban areas across the United States. By federal policy. "Employment assistance" via on-
the-job training and work experience, direct job placement, and limited help in urban living were provided to Native relocatees. The purpose was the implementation of the U.S.
government's goal of assimilation and acculturation—the effect and result saw Indian
people facing and undergoing changes from their Native identity into "modern Americans."

Change, change, change—the stories of California were now enriched with Indians facing urban relocation in California (at the same time, Indians were relocated to other urban
areas across the nation—Chicago, Illinois; Denver, Colorado; Dallas, Texas; Cleveland,
Ohio). Oakland was one of the main relocation destinations, and that Acoma Pueblo song
could very well have been sung by 1960s Acoma relocatees to Oakland, or by the 1930s to
1950s Acoma people who'd gone to work for the railroad at nearby Richmond, where a
worker colony was located.

If there is anything this book is expressive of, it is the insistence that Native people will
be who they are as *Indians* living in urban communities, Natives thriving as cultural people
strong in Indian ethnicity, and Natives helping each other socially, spiritually, economically,
and politically no matter what. I lived in the Bay Area in 1975–79 and 1986–87, and I was
always struck by the Native (many people do say "American Indian" emphatically!) community and by a cultural identity that has always insisted on being second to none! Yes, indeed, this book is a dynamic, living document and tribute to the Oakland Indian community as well as to the Bay Area Indian community as a whole.

INTRODUCTION

This is a book about our community, the Bay Area Indian community, with a particular emphasis on the past seventy years. It offers the words, the images, and some of the thinking that comes from the community. This is not a book that takes a scholarly approach or analyzes the community, but rather it is a book *of* the community: a reflection and documentation of the history of some of the people and significant places, events, and activities that make up and shape the community. Many of the words recorded in the oral histories, the written pieces prepared especially for this book, the photographic and artistic images, and even the fliers, posters, and news clippings hold deep and rich connotations for those of us who have participated in the Indian community over the years. This book is a sharing of some of that experience of participation.

The Bay Area Indian community is multitribal, made of Native people and their descendants—those who originate here and those who have come to the Bay region from all over the United States and from other parts of this hemisphere. Although some places are significant to us here, the community itself is not fundamentally a place, but rather a network of relatedness, of people linked to one another because of family, tribe, shared experiences, and shared understandings about those experiences. Some have said, "We are all family" or "We are the urban tribe," and this is a part of what we mean when we say "all my relations."

This book has been long in the making, and many people have contributed to its creation. Like most things in our community, it has come about at its own pace, giving us all time to think about how we can best give it the right shape and texture in order to make it a clear and strong reflection of the Bay Area Indian community. In 1976, Gerri Martinez Lira, Marilyn St. Germaine, Susan Lobo, and others began talking about the need to begin documenting the life stories and thoughts of the Elders, in particular those of various tribes who had come into the Bay Area via the Bureau of Indian Affairs Relocation Program and earlier, and who had been active and instrumental in creating and sustaining the community. Gerri and Marilyn, both social workers, were the codirectors of the social services department at Intertribal Friendship House (IFH) in the mid-1970s. Susan was the non-Indian wife in an Indian family, and her young daughter was involved in IFH activities. She was trained as an anthropologist with a background in doing oral histories.

These discussions took place at IFH—the Oakland Indian Center—which is the oldest and one of the principal Indian organizations in the area. (In fact, IFH and the Chicago Indian Center, both established in the 1950s during the early years of relocation, are the oldest still-operating urban Indian organizations in the United States.) These discussions evolved into the creation of the Community History Project at IFH in 1976. Soon Joyce Keoke, Sharon Bennett, and Charlene Betsillie joined in, and all six came to be the Community History Project board as well as the editorial committee of this book.

We all realized that the history and contemporary makeup of the Bay Area Indian community was unique but in some ways also parallel and similar to other urban Indian communities, such as those found in Minneapolis, Chicago, Seattle, Los Angeles, Phoenix, Denver, Dallas, and New York. Some of the urban communities throughout the United States grew during the relocation years of the 1950s and 1960s, whereas others have distinct historical roots. We know that some of the personal histories and thoughts expressed here will be familiar to many Indian people throughout the United States, reflecting their own lives; we also know that in reading these pages many may personally identify with the topics covered, may actually know some of the people interviewed, and may even have participated in some of the events described in the book.

We also realized that people, especially non-Indian people, not involved in these communities were very frequently oblivious to the very existence of Indians in the city. Compared to the vast amount of written work regarding Indians in historical contexts and within specific cultural traditions, very little has been written about contemporary Indian urban experiences and almost nothing in the voices of those who have lived those experiences. We searched the social science literature—almost nothing; fiction—almost no mention of Indians living in urban areas; the popular press, media, and journalism—an occasional sensational and usually negative stereotype–laden account. Gerri, Marilyn, and Sharon on the editorial committee and others who work to provide services of all types within the Indian community have been confronted on a daily basis with the profoundly negative effects of the Indian community's "invisibility" to the population at large, including those people in federal, state, and local agencies, and those who might otherwise potentially fund and support Indian service programs and other activities. An urban Indian community countered all existing mainstream stereotypes: "Indians in cities, no way!" (Whispered and hardly ever said directly to one's face.) "But I thought all Indian people lived on reservations in rural areas or . . . were dead."

The Community History Project was not begun initially to address the need to educate the people outside the Indian community, but more immediately to answer the need in the community to document the words of the Elders and to honor those who had established and shaped the community. The project was begun with an emphasis on taped and transcribed oral histories, and it received funding from the Rosenberg Foundation, the American Friends Service Committee, and later the California Council for the Humanities and the LEF Foundation, among others. As time went on and as families began to donate photographs and other family and community documents and memorabilia, the project that had begun with oral histories evolved into an archive that also now includes more than eleven thousand photographs, extensive files of documents, fliers, more than one thousand posters, music, and audio- and videotapes—all with a focus on the Bay Area Indian community. This collection we came to call the Community Resource Archives because it continues to be of the Indian community, located in the community at IFH, under the control of the community, and accessible to community members as well as to others. Although it is a small collection by some standards, we believe it to be the only such archive in the United States that is community based and that focuses on an urban Indian community.

Joyce, Susan, and many others have worked for many years in the Community History Project office and archives at IFH. Since the Community History Project was established, it has been not only a repository of the documentation of the history of the Bay Area Indian community, but also a resource that provides materials for working on community-based calendars, newsletters, murals, and radio programs, as well as for working with youth in the community and with Indian and non-Indian students from the University of California at Berkeley, San Francisco State University, and Mills College on video and other research projects. The Community History Project has provided information for fund-raising in the community overall and for many years has been part of the annual IFH music festivals. Through the project, technical training, work experience, workshops, and conferences have been offered. It has made materials and resources available for research by families and by students and scholars. Materials were loaned to a number of exhibits on a national level, and a number of photographic exhibits were created, some of which traveled. A permanent photographic exhibit on display at IFH since 1990 includes photographs and oral history quotes selected by a careful committee process. Many of these same photographs and quotes provide the core of this book.

Since the beginning of the Community History Project, the idea of a book kept surfacing. We often heard the question, "Hey, when's that book coming out?" It emerged slowly, and as time went on we began to put aside materials that people in the community said would be good to include. The book that you hold in your hands draws deeply from this collection, with thorough and broad-based consideration over many years. By 1990, the book had become an active focus, and we were talking seriously with the University of Arizona Press about publishing it. As a result of our agreement with the Press, all earnings from the sale of this book will go directly to support the programs and activities at IFH.

This book is organized into five semichronological parts: "The Beginnings," "Relocation," "Building Community," "Times of Change," and "Creating a Community for Future Generations."

In "The Beginnings," the stage is set for introducing the Bay Area environment, and as Darryl Wilson tells in his "Time Line," "The elders said, 'this place where we dwell today was made. It is beautiful, this place, because the song is beautiful.'" This first part continues to introduce some of the diversity of experiences and Indian Peoples who came into the Bay Area up until the mid-1900s: the young men and women who came in the 1930s and 1940s after leaving boarding school, those who were in the military, or who made their way into the city from more rural areas of northern California. Mention is made of the Four Winds Club, one of the first Indian-focused organizations in the Bay Area, and of the special arrangement between Acoma and Laguna Pueblos and the Santa Fe Railroad through which the Santa Fe Indian Village was established.

As part 2, "Relocation," tells, the federal Relocation Program was established in the early 1950s and created a surge of new migration into the Bay Area by Native Peoples from throughout the United States. Oakland, San Francisco, and San Jose were some of the first cities earmarked as relocation sites by this program, which was aimed at moving Indian people off their land and assimilating them into the mainstream. This part contrasts, via news clippings, the optimistic bureaucratic relocation aims with the complex and varied experiences of Indian people themselves. The themes of longing, despair, hopefulness, and exhilaration are expressed in the writing of Peggy Berryhill and Yvonne Lamore-Choate, while the art, the poetry, oral history quotes, and photographs give a picture of the early years of struggle to adapt to city living and to establish a multitribal urban Indian community. The continuity of this community with roots in relocation is expressed in the writing and photographs of the families and children of the original relocatees as they acknowledge their parents' often heroic efforts to create community and to maintain the strength of family in a place so far from home.

"Building Community," part 3, tells of the many ways that Indian people came together to build a community, a network of relatedness, and of the many clubs, organizations, events, and activities that gave meaning to a new urban way of life. In this part, some of the people who were particularly crucial during the early days, such as Walter Lasley, are acknowledged and honored. It also highlights the issues to be dealt with in the city, including problems with the law and alcoholism, and mentions the creation of solutions specific to Indian ways and needs. It shows some of the ways Indian people in the city come together to have fun—at the pow-wows, through sports, during the holidays—and always doing it, as Marilyn St. Germaine writes, with that special deep appreciation of life and with Indian humor. Children, families, relations all have a voice in this part. As Melinda Sanderson says, everyone in "the community, from the Elders down to the children . . . is like my family."

"Times of Change," part 4, tells of the social and political awareness that moved Indian people to action in the 1960s and 1970s. The Bay Area—with the occupation of Alcatraz, the initiation of the Long Walk, and the creation of the Survival School, among many other events—was a region whose thinking and actions had far-reaching effects nationally, many of which continue today. These actions of solidarity and demands for justice found expression not only in demonstrations and political movements but also in creative expressions, in the pictorial arts, in music, and in radio and film, as Janeen Antoine describes. The voices of leaders such as Bill Wahpepah are heard in this part, and the activities of the American Indian Movement and the International Indian Treaty Council are expressed here in words, photographs, and graphic art. Woven throughout is the reemergence and assertion of the strong spiritual base that underlies Native life.

In part 5, "Creating a Community for Future Generations," the emphasis is on the children and younger generation of the Bay Area Indian community. By the 1990s, a third generation was growing up, the grandchildren of those who had originally relocated to the area. Their lives and thinking is reflected in this part: from their participation in the American Indian Preschool—later known as Hintil Kuu Ca, the American Indian Charter School—to their street action and even their parenthood. Ramona Wilson writes of the community's many sustained educational efforts. By the time of this urban generation, not only is the community multitribal, but many people are also multitribal—grounded both in the city and back home, both in a modern way and in a traditional way. Both Julian Lang and Tasina Ska Win write of the many linkages between homelands and the city life, and Esther G. Belin, in "Blues-ing on the Brown Vibe," gives us a sense of modern urban life as "Coyote struts down East 14th" in Oakland. Once again everything is tied together by family and by the knowledge that passes from one generation to the next.

For those who wish to read more about some of the topics in this book, we have appended two bibliographies of additional readings, both those specific to the Bay Area and those of a more national scope.

This book, then, is the result of many years and the active contribution of many, many people—not only the more than ninety people whose words are found here and whose photographs and flier art and posters appear here, but also those who over the last twenty-five years have assisted in building the Community History Project archives through their contributions of time, energy, and materials. All of these caring and thoughtful people in our community have made this book possible by offering their support and encouragement, and by sharing their hearts and spirit. This book has also been deeply shaped by all those conversations on the sofas in IFH's living room or at the dining tables after the Wednesday Night Dinner, conversations often laced with the loose comment, "That book had better include . . ." or "That's my cousin in that photo; here's where you can reach her." To

all of these many hundreds of people who assisted to make this book a reality, we are deeply grateful. In addition, we extend our thanks to the American Friends Service Committee and to the current IFH board of directors for the many ways they have contributed their support and ideas to our efforts: Gary Hodge (chair), Stephanie Lindsey (secretary), Andrew Hayes, Tom Burbank, Harkin Lucero Jr., Crystal K. Salas, and Sonny Sixkiller. To everyone, too numerous to name, who participated in even the smallest way, we offer our respect and our thanks for sharing in the creation of this, our community book.

—*Editorial Committee: Susan Lobo, Marilyn LaPlante St. Germaine, Sharon Mitchell Bennett, Gerri Lira, Charlene Betsillie, Joyce Keoke (not pictured)*

PART ONE THE BEGINNINGS

California Indian people have always been in what is now the San Francisco Bay Area. Traveling, trading, and intermarriage linked people of this immediate area with those more distant. These links continue today, but by the 1930s and 1940s a series of events took place that began to attract Indian migrants from more distant places. This was the beginning of the intertribal basis of the American Indian community in the Bay Area.

Many American Indians in the armed forces during the First and Second World Wars were stationed in the Bay Area. Others came to work in war-related industries. Some chose to stay. During the same period, students at boarding schools such as Inter-mountain or the Sherman Institute in Riverside often worked during the summers or after graduation in the homes of families living in the Bay Area. As Indian people searched out one another, existing organizations such as the YWCA were focal points for meeting. Eventually, these first migrants to the city formed clubs such as the Four Winds. Many people who came to the Bay Area during the 1930s and 1940s were young and unmarried, and planned to stay only a short time. Some eventually returned home to rural areas and reservations, but some did stay in the city and became the founding generation of the Bay Area American Indian community.

Time Line

Darryl Babe Wilson

It is said by my tribal people of ancient knowledge that the universe is a vastness filled with many galaxies, all turning to the Song that created them long ago, each in rhythm with the other, listing in their great churning orbits—orbits that were put into motion by the Great Mysteries when they decided to stir the vastness with a huge yet invisible *jup'elo* (canoe paddle), causing all of the content of that Song to whirl in continuous motion.

In that forever swirling, the galaxies meander away from each other in their ever-expanding motion, seeking to touch forever. All that we know and all that we cannot know were created at that stirring motion. However, it took millions of ages for the power within the stars to create their own songs, causing earths and moons to appear. And they did, it is said, for we are here.

By a beautiful song, our little Earth was brought into being, water everywhere. At first it was Kwaw (Silver Gray Fox). He sang for a million years or more and created an island. Then it was Kwaw, Annikadel (Wise Lizard), Et'wi Minu (Eagle Woman, who was, in the beginning, Cloud Maiden), Aleum (Frog Woman), and Jp'hesset (Hummingbird). And Ma'ka'ta (Old Man Coyote) was there, too, plotting. This creative process took millions of years of singing. The Elders said, "This place where we dwell today was made. It is beautiful, this place, because the song is beautiful."

So an island was created from a song, and the island was floating upon the vast water. Magic was everywhere. Mountains, storms, forests, rivers, animals, moon, mornings and sunsets, fruit and flowers were made. Then people were sung into being by Kwaw.

And the people were taught by the great powers to live, to hunt and fish, and to explore the beautiful earth, and they did.

Sun and Stars watched as little Earth took great powers and "came to herself." She traveled the vastness with Moon.

At a place now known as California much of Earth's singing and creating began, then continued throughout all of the land. In the very far south, the Inca constructed grand temples of worship and

3

ALL MY RELATIONS:
WE CHANGE, BUT WE ARE THE SAME

Our Grandparents, Crow
Children, 1910–1916.

Our Children, Jenny and Toby
James at the American Indian
Preschool, Oakland, 1972.

grand societies, and they were brilliant people who dreamed dreams. In the far north, the Snow People learned how to take from the great sea the huge fish—fish as big as a small mountain. They, too, were dreamers, it is said. In the land of beautiful birds and soft days, the people sang songs of greatness, and they made their dreams appear as huge pyramids rising from vast forests, and today they dream of greater accomplishments tomorrow.

Also in other lands people dreamed and made their dreams appear. Often they wondered, and it took many seasons, but their songs also appeared in the physical form that they thought them to be.

As the Hopi people were preparing to emerge from the First World, they heard the great thundering as the mountains fell into the outer ocean. Quetzalcoatl was put out of his homeland by a jealous mob of lords and governors because he held the needs of the people paramount in his thoughts and dreams, and their needs were met. Exiled, he traveled to the east on a raft made of serpents, some say, to become Wa'loo'lolei (Morning Star), promising to return with a vengeance one day. It was five thousand more snows before the creation of the Chilam Balam of Chumayel and six thousand summers before the first basket of earth began the construction of Tenochtitlán.

The Great Pyramid of Cholula and the Sphinx of Egypt were still dreams, and the Great Wall of China was only an idea. The Champs Élysées waited for more than a thousand years before the first brick was laid. The glorious people of Australia met upon a great plain and danced. The great tribes of the Black Continent sang sweet songs to sweet Gods and sweet Life, and they flourished. The Golden Horde of Asia was not yet thought of, and it would be some time before Conquering and Assimilating were concepts of the nervous tribes of northern Europe.

One day, the Elders say, there was an angry rumbling deep in Earth. The whole world shook. There was a great and painful breaking—broken bone grating against broken bone—and the mountains in the west fell off into the outer ocean, and terrifying waves were everywhere. Earth wobbled in its orbit. Mis Misa, the little power that dwells within AkoYet (Mt. Shasta) and balances the earth with the universe, made the proper adjustments, and we continued our journey.

That was when the San Joaquin Valley and the Sacramento Valley were one solid freshwater lake, "as long as the land." When the mountains fell into the sea, the salt waters thundered in, and the fresh waters surged out. There was a huge clash of wills, each wanting to "best" the other until there was an adjustment, a calming. And there in the aftermath of tremendous forces was the beautiful bay, which is now known as the San Francisco Bay. Soon the people went to see what was there. They left footprints in the sand, large ones and very small ones, side by side. It was good. They stayed. And they sang and danced to all of the powers of the universe.

"The Dancer"

Midnight

One night while I was looking
out the window, I heard the moon
calling my name

The moon said, "Come up here with
me and we can dance with the stars."

—Taweah Garcia, Mono/Pit River, Grade 5

Indian Life in the City: A Glimpse of the Urban Experience of Pomo Women in the 1930s

Victoria D. Patterson

It was from this rural, mostly impoverished Indian settlement [Hopland in northern California] that Frances Jack went to Oakland to get a job. She went down to the "city" on the general advice of her mother, who wanted her to have more of a chance in life than she thought she would get in Ukiah. She went to the Oakland YWCA on the specific advice of a friend who had worked in the city and who gave her instructions and the name of a contact person at the Y.

. . . Most of the girls [who contacted Mildred Van Every at the YWCA Placement Services] were placed as maids, whose jobs were to "dust, clean, cook, and take care of children." "We have jobs," said Van Every, "only for girls. The boys can't get jobs down here." . . . Although work was plentiful and a regular paycheck welcome, life in the city had its dark side. "It's awful lonesome not knowing anyone down here," wrote a Pomo girl. "This morning when I woke I felt like packing my bags and going back home to Ukiah." The reality of working life was also very hard. The steady pace and the separation from family and friends were painful for the many Pomo women living in isolated job sites among strangers.

One of the official clubs formed by the Oakland Y was the Four Winds Club for Indians. It provided a central meeting place for Indians away from home in Oakland through the Second World

War. "That's where you meet all the boys and girls and make friends," said a Pomo girl.

Frances Jack remembers that every Thursday, the working girls' day off, "everyone" (that is, other Indians working in the Bay Area, including out-of-state Indians) would go downtown to the Y, to the Four Winds Club. Once a month the girls would give a dinner and dance for the Indian boys going to the university at Berkeley. At the time she was there, 1936, there were six Indian boys at Cal. At Christmas time, there would be a party and a dance hosted by out-of-state Indians. The Y, too, developed a tradition of delivering Christmas baskets to Indians living in Oakland. The Four Winds Club eventually developed into Oakland's Intertribal Friendship House, which continues to be a center for Indian activities in the Bay Area.

Other Indian women were frustrated by their attempts to leave domestic work for other employment. Sherman Institute prepared them only for domestic work. A few Pomo women enrolled in a nursing course, which most had to abandon owing to lack of funds. Some others in 1940 enrolled at Merritt Business College to obtain secretarial training. They had part-time employment through Van Every [at the Y].

In the end, though, the desire to be home among family and friends prevailed over the possibility of better wages. This is evidenced by the continual coming and going between Oakland and Hopland, Ukiah, Lakeport, and elsewhere. . . . Most girls chose to jeopardize their jobs every summer by returning to Mendocino County for the hop season, that time of riverside trysts, easy living, and wages that equaled ten months of dreary housework in someone else's house. The combination of city work in the winter and hop season at home in the summer provided an excellent annual income and the best of both worlds.

I believe that the primary reason young Pomo women returned home is that they preferred it to city life. They chose to return not in defeat, but in conscious preference. As young girls craving change and excitement, they exploited the city environment for its novelty, its education, its money, and its good times, and when it was time to settle down, have children, and get serious, home was the place to live. . . . Francis Jack went back to Hopland Rancheria in 1949 after training as a nurse and building airplane engines in

Sacramento (a job she loved, by the way). She returned to marry and to become the first tribal chairperson of Hopland's new government, organized after the group's landmark legal challenge to termination, in which she played a prominent part. She became a well-known writer and bilingual educator, fluent in many dialects of Central Pomo as well as in other Pomo languages. She actively fought the ubiquitous local racism that continues in Ukiah.

"I was born in Laguna Pueblo in 1910. Then I went to school there to sixth grade. There was no other high school there at that time, so I had to leave home. I came to Riverside, California, to Sherman Institute. Then I was there until I graduated. From there I did go home for a while, so I could be with my parents. But I couldn't find any work, so I returned to Los Angeles. So I went back and notified the BIA [Bureau of Indian Affairs] there, and they placed me in a home to work for a family. In the meantime, I applied for an educational vocational loan, and it took me three years to get that. Then they enrolled me at Frank Wiggins Trade School, and I went there and finished the course there in dressmaking, alterations, and all that. Then I finished, but at that time it was right in the middle of the Depression, you know, and I couldn't find any work after that, so I just remained with this family for a while. They let you know that you were just the help there. You could never ever get involved with them. They had their own kind of social life, so you could never feel at home with them. You feel like you don't belong there. That's the way I always felt. And you work from morning to night. And then you have to work so hard there; you get no hours, you know. I took care of the children and the cooking, housework, and everything, all the heavy laundry. Sometimes you feel . . . you just fall in bed at night. Some people, they expect you to work every minute that you were in the house. That's the reason, to this day, I hate housework—because on account of that, I guess. One day [off a week] and maybe every other Sunday. And if they're good, they'll let you off every Sunday. And such small pay. I started out with about thirty dollars a month. Then I moved up here [to Oakland] and we got married."

—*Ethel Rogoff*

"[During the summer when I was at Intermountain boarding school] I came here to Oakland. Most of my friends were coming down to Oakland, so I came down, too. It was a doctor's family in Oakland. I was to go and live with them. They had two little kids I had to take care of. I stayed with them all summer. I don't have to do cooking for them; just take care of the little kids, take care of the house, and ironing. They were just like parents to me. They took me a lot of places. The doctor was a member of the country club, so we used to go there swimming, picnic a lot. I decided to come back the following year. They treat me nice. She asked me not to call her Mrs. Winslow. She said, "Call me 'Auntie.'" So I called her "Auntie." And then after I graduated, I wanted to come back again, so I stayed with the same family. They treated me a lot better than the first time I came down. They always introduced me to their friends and family, and I was like one member of the family. [Her] sister, her niece, and her nephew, they used to call me "Cousin." I never did went home. I stayed out here since then. Three years I stayed with the Winslow family. [Then] they found me a place; they worried about it. She paid my rent at a hotel somewhere in Oakland. I was like one of her daughters. She paid my room and board for three months. I got a job. I liked the idea of being on my own. I was eighteen."
—*Helen Stanley*

"The active work was to get young people going on to school. I must say that from 1934 to 1942 we had a very able group of young people who came down from northern Nevada and northern California and went to the old Oakland Central Trade School. They were very good in carpentry, very good in welding. The other group went to the Merritt School of Business—machine sewing and cooking. But that was part of the work that I did, which was to get them into the different schools, to work up their credentials so that they could be accepted. Mostly [they came] from boarding schools. Quite a group came from up at Hupa and Smith River. I'm thinking of two young people who went to San Francisco State in child care, and there are several that went into nurses' training.

"The YWCA always provided sleeping quarters for the young people when they came down. The boys would always get quarters in the YMCA. They [the Four Winds Club] met Thursdays; that was the day off for household employees. Then once a month they would have the big dances."

—*Mildred Van Every*

(Mildred Van Every was the sole social worker in the Bay Area employed by the Bureau of Indian Affairs and placed at the Oakland YWCA from 1934 to 1942. The office was then moved to San Francisco, where she stayed until 1952.)

"I came out here on my own; no experience or anything. That was in '34. You know, when I was on the bus coming, I never did get out of Oklahoma before that. That was during the war, everybody coming out here for the jobs. So we had to go to Richmond. So that morning it was foggy and cold. I heard that you could go here, and there was sunshine all year round, and it wasn't like that. So I just like to freeze to death when I came and didn't bring any . . . I just brought the one big trunk, just a few blankets and a few clothes. When I came out here, I had to do two weeks' training for electrician. That was the only thing that was open at the shipyards, and so I went to school in two weeks, and they got me a job in the shipyards. I was working there as a helper, you know. But when the war was calmed down or whatever it was, they laid off lots of people."

—*Alice Carnes*

"[In those days] it was more individual families—because it was these women that stayed in the Bay Area and got married and raised families. They made it on their own. When relocation started, more services were offered. The men, like my father, came into the area right after the First World War. He was recruited right from his hometown. Then he started working in construction in the Bay Area and California. Later, during World War II, he worked at Treasure Island for the U.S. navy. He eventually retired."

—*Coralee Willis*

Euro-American Womanhood Ceremony

Esther G. Belin

Some say the boarding school experience wasn't that bad
because they learned a trade
at least the men did

The women
they were trained to specialize in domestic household work
to mimic the rituals of Euro-American women
to cook roast beef and not mutton
to eat white bread and not frybread
to start a family and not an education
to be happy servants to doctors' families in Sierra Madre
and then to their own

The young women who never really became women because they
    were taken off the rez before they could go through a
    womanhood ceremony
the young women who adapted to the Euro-American version of
    a womanhood ceremony

Instead of fasting and sweating and praying and running
They set the table and vacuumed and ironed and nursed and fed
and gave birth and birth and birth to a new nation of
    mixedbloods
and urban Indians
And they were mothers/providers/wives
They were strong and loved and made love and sobered up
and organized weekend road trips back to the rez
Back to the rez where we all came from
and where we need to return
to heal our wounds
from the Euro-American womanhood ceremony.

"Before we were married, I used to work for the Telephone Company, and so I always passed the YWCA and seeing people coming and going. So one time I went in. In those days [the late 1930s], they were having all social gatherings once a month for the service people, and I'd go in and see what they were doing, and got acquainted with [Indian] people there. That was my only social life. I didn't know of any other way of going about it. I never was one to go to bars or dance halls or anything. I'd meet some of the Indian people, and they'd say, 'Why don't you come up to the Y?' So I'd go up there after work to have some social dancing. They had dances once or twice a month. After we got married [in 1944], we'd go for that and got active into the programs, help them plan programs and things like that. Then the war was over, around '45, '46, and then more families started coming, instead of single people. So we got really active in that. In the very beginning, the Four Winds Club, it was supposed to be for working girls from reservations or from the schools. They brought them down here to work in homes, in rich people's home. They always got Thursdays off, and so then they would have Thursday afternoon [at the Four Winds Club] for all the girls to get together and sew or go to shows or do something together. It was one way they were trying to keep control of them, too, so they wouldn't be running off to the bars and places they shouldn't be going. I understand that it was way back in 1924 when the Four Winds Club started. [In the 1950s], it probably outgrew itself. Intertribal House came and was starting up, and it probably drew a lot of our people from Four Winds there because it was what the people needed then. It was a place to go more than once a week. They were open three or four nights a week. They had Sunday services and Saturday activities."

—*Genny Mitchell*

"I had three choices after that training. I had a chance to go to Korea, to Japan, to Hawaii, and then to Treasure Island. Of course, hearing something about Treasure Island, in the back of my mind I figured it must be an island somewhere with all the luxuries. So I decided to go to Treasure Island. Then I noticed that it was in the San Francisco Bay Area."

—*Al Hicks*

THE NEWS MEDIA: FOUR WINDS CLUB PROGRAM.

Oakland Tribune

EXCLUSIVE ASSOCIATED PRESS...WIREPHOTO...WIDE WORLD...UNITED PRESS

VOL. CXLI   OAKLAND, CALIFORNIA, MONDAY, DEC. 18, 1944   13   C   NO. 171

MEATS, FATS a
   points each, v
USED FATS—Eac
GASOLINE—A cc
   C4, B5 and C3
PROCESSED FO
   points each, v
SHOES—"Airplane
SUGAR—Stamps
   five pounds, h

Outfitted with ceremonial dancing feathers, these two Indians—White Buffalo (left), Cheyenne, and A. J. Hunt, Pueblo—helped entertain servicemen at the Y.W.C.A. here

Coralie Eddards of the Ute and Cherokee tribes dances to the tom-tom played by Barrie Harris, Hopi Indian, at an entertainment present here last night for servicemen.

These regal chiefs are members of the Four Winds Club, sponsored by the Y.W.C.A., which presented a Christmas party for servicemen last night. They are (left to right), David Eddards, Cherokee; Albert C. Frank and James Edsitty, Navajos. Indian dances were demonstrated. Most of the Indians participating are shipyard workers.—Tribune photos.

The Santa Fe Indian Village

Ruth Sarracino Hopper

Today, Indian life is a combination of urban and rural. Before, if you stayed away for months from your reservation, people thought you had become a city Indian, a concrete Indian. And, for most Indians, it is hard to live in the city because you miss your home, and you are trying to deal with all the situations like relocation in the old days and, now, just your choice to be here. As for my sister and me, we feel we were lucky to be able to be raised here in the Bay Area, but in a setting exactly like back home. Because our father worked out here for the Atchison, Topeka, and Santa Fe Railroad, we kind of had no choice. Where we lived was called the Santa Fe Indian Village, right outside the city limits—or should I say jurisdiction—of Richmond, California. It was like the rez. The city of Richmond really had no say about the land that we lived on. I am Laguna. My people came this far away, two states away, beginning in 1922, which was way before the Relocation Program happened in the 1950s. Our people came here because of an agreement with the railroad that because the tracks went through our land, we would get jobs working on the railroad, and they would provide us with housing at some of the railheads. We brought our government, just like at home. We had a council of officers; our parents all spoke our language; we held our dances, had our outdoor ovens, and planted our fields here with corn, melons, and other crops. Our men went deer hunting, and we had traditional deer dinners and deer dancing: the whole works! Oh, yeah! Our parents made sure we had the living style of home.

After relocation started in the 1950s, our people would invite friends from other tribes to come to some of our activities in the village. And around about that time, the Intertribal Friendship House emerged. It was a good place for gathering and welcoming for all the Indian people. I remember they had rock-and-roll dances, or American dances as the older people called them. Then later there was the American Indian Center in San Francisco on Sixteenth and Mission. The American dances were held in Oakland on Friday night and in San Francisco on Saturday nights. There was also the YMCA off Broadway in downtown Oakland. These were the hot spots in those days—other than the seven bars called Indian

Tom Ahmie, first governor
for the Laguna people at Santa Fe
Indian village, 1942.

Ruth Sarracino (Hopper),
Victor Sarracino, and Joanne Sarracino
in front of their house.

Ruth Sarracino (Hopper), her mother,
and sister, Joanne, in front of their house
at the Santa Fe Indian Village.

Joanne at home, 1950s.

bars, which weren't actually owned by Indians, except one later on. Then the Bay Area Indian Council developed and played a good part in the support of the community centers, hosted an annual pow-wow every year and started the Bay Area Princess contest. Then after the Bureau of Indian Affairs offices left Alameda County and moved to Sacramento, a lot of different agencies developed here. Does that tell you anything? But, over the years, from what I have seen come and go, and through the good times and bad, I do congratulate all the people who have taken part and contributed time and efforts to the development of all the Indian organizations and agencies we now have for all our people here in the city and off the rez. Your work is appreciated and acknowledged.

Feast Day, Santa Fe Indian Village, 1954. Beatrice V. Sanchez and her daughter, Evangeline Sanchez Felipe.

"My Dad came in '39 because he was hired by the Santa Fe Railroad. There were two tribes here then, Acoma and Laguna. They provided them with housing and a job. This was like an exchange since the railroad had gone through our land. They built a village there in the Santa Fe rail yards. They got boxcars and added rooms to them. I grew up there in what was called Richmond Indian Village [Santa Fe Indian Village]. At that time, there were about one hundred families altogether. We built our ovens and made our traditional oven bread. Certain times of the year we did our traditional dances. We had our own officers that ran the village. My grandfather retired from the railroad. So did my dad. Now my husband works for the railroad."

—*Shirley J. Medina, daughter of Beatrice V. Sanchez*

THE NEWS MEDIA: FEAST DAY FOR SERVICE VETERANS DURING WWII.

Four Winds Club In YWCA Affair
Indians Enjoy Turkey

PACIFIC VETERAN—Glenn Howard, navy veteran of 24 months in the Pacific, member of Pima tribe of American Indians, really enjoys turkey as members of Four Winds club, American Indian organization, hold Thanksgiving dinner at Y.W.C.A. Frances Johnson of Cherokee tribe looks on.

SOLDIERS ENJOY "FEED"—Among the 100 or more American Indians at the Four Winds club dinner were these soldiers: Juanita Poulton (standing) of Mono tribe serves, left to right: Allen Hunt, Pueblo tribe; Pfc. Frank Luther, Navajo tribe, and Pfc. Laurence Claremont, Sioux tribe.

Wedding of Mr. and Mrs. Palmer Duncan, December 26, 1956.

INTER-TRIBAL FRIENDSHIP HOUSE

PART TWO RELOCATION

By 1954, Indian people from many parts of the United States began arriving in the Bay Area through the federal Relocation Program. Although aspects of the program changed over the years, most typically those who relocated were granted transportation to an urban area, some initial assistance for housing for a few months, and possibly assistance in finding jobs. In later years, job training was added. For many, the move into the city was lonely and frightening, like stepping off into the unknown, and actual arrival was often a sudden jolt of urban reality. The assistance of a few months' duration provided by the Relocation Program was inadequate to meet the often complex, diverse, and immense survival needs of people who found themselves initially in an alien environment, often far from home, their extended families, and tribal territories.

After the swell of migration into the Bay Area began in the 1950s, more Indian people arrived. Some had been in boarding schools together. Relatives joined family groups. A series of organizations were established by Indian people or in conjunction with other organizations such as the American Friends Service Committee. These Indian organizations have served as nodes in the communitywide network, providing the means for gaining basic food, health, and education services; for pursuing economic stability; and for achieving cultural and spiritual expression. They are the places where people from many different tribes gather to create new traditions, to provide mutual support, to exchange information and ideas, to take care of communitywide business, and also just to get together and have fun. Through them, Indians in the Bay Area have found ways to validate tribal identity, while simultaneously building an intertribal, urban community identity. In the years following relocation, communitywide activities such as pow-wows and sports league events began to take place.

Relocation: The Promise and the Lie

Ray Moisa

California is home to more than 250,000 Native Americans [2000 Census, 333, 346], the largest Indian population of any state. Yet fewer than 12 percent are Native Californians. The rest of us, almost 178,000 in number, do not consider California our true home.

We are the relocatees or their children and grandchildren. We are the beneficiaries, or victims, of the Bureau of Indian Affairs (BIA) Relocation Program of the 1950s. As a result of this program, which one writer has called "the largest forced migration in history," an estimated quarter of a million Native Americans left their reservation homes, with the BIA's assistance and coercion, in search of greater economic opportunity in the cities.

But was relocation truly a forced migration, a modern-day equivalent of the "Longest Walk" endured by so many tribes in the nineteenth century? Relocation was, after all, completely voluntary. It was established as a way of helping Indian people who wanted to escape the poverty of reservation life for jobs and an education in the cities.

Besides, official policy did not prevent anyone from returning to their reservations. Many Indian people did, in fact, return, forsaking Washington's glittering promise of an easier city life for the spiritual comfort of home. Estimates provided at several urban relocation centers indicate a return rate of up to 60 percent in the early years. The BIA's official figures acknowledge high return rates of 35 percent in 1953, 30 percent in 1954, and 28 percent in 1955.

This historical record, unfortunately, contains very little material on relocation. The Community History Project at Intertribal Friendship House in Oakland, California, has on file oral histories from a number of the early relocatees, and a few books have been published containing a smattering of information on the subject.

The literature that is available paints a very complex picture of the program. The opinions differ widely with regard to the program's successes and failures, the official objectives and hidden agendas, and the promises and the lies. It is an intriguing and often tragic story born of well-intentioned, naive idealism married to insidious bureaucratic irresponsibility. In the end, once again, many Indian people suffered greatly as a result of the BIA's ineptitude.

The relocation story has its beginnings in the late 1940s—a heady time for America. The nation was victorious in war, self-righteous, and filled with a sense of its own unbridled destiny. We had "Give 'Em Hell" Harry in the White House, the Marshall Plan in Europe, and the Pax Americana all over the world. And in California, a freshman congressman named Richard Nixon was making national headlines investigating "un-American activities." It was the beginning of an era of strict conformity throughout the United States.

The BIA was not immune to the mood infecting the nation. Bureau policymakers, most notably Commissioner of Indian Affairs Dillon Myer, interpreted the popular sentiment as a mandate to bring Indians into mainstream society on a massive scale. In doing so, Myer and other bureaucrats reversed more than a century of conventional wisdom in the bureau. Unlike most programs originating out of the BIA, the new goals were patently destructive of Indian traditional values centered around tribalism and the support of reservation life.

The four gospels according to Myer were termination, relocation, assimilation, and acculturation. Throughout the late 1940s and early 1950s, numerous congressional hearings were held. As the hearings progressed, the policymakers' intent became clear: to dissolve the special trust relationship between Indians and the federal government. Time after time, the same themes were echoed in the government's testimony: do away with tribal recognition, break up the reservation system, and dismantle the BIA.

At the heart of this effort was the government's desire to rid itself once and for all of "the Indian problem" that would not go away. It was felt the best way to do this was to unilaterally declare an end to all federal responsibility to the Indian, while at the same time enticing thousands to leave their reservations with the promise of jobs and a better life in the cities. The policymakers wanted to believe the Indian people would blend into the landscape of urban anonymity and disappear forever in a faceless crowd of overwhelming numbers. Once that goal was achieved, America would no longer have to face the constant reminders of its gross mistreatment of Indian people.

It was no accident that Myer was chosen commissioner of Indian Affairs at this time. During World War II, Myer had been director of the War Relocation Authority, the agency responsible for uprooting from their homes tens of thousands of Americans of Japanese descent and herding them off to concentration camps or "relocation centers" in the California desert.

Myer's ruthless expertise, coupled with the greed and avarice of the big power, timber, and land interests who stood to profit from the breakup of the reservations, combined to form a near-deadly combination for the Indian. The result was the Relocation-Vocational Training Act, first proposed in 1948 and enacted in 1951.

The basic objectives of the act were twofold and, on the face of it, deceptively benign. One aspect of the program provided employment assistance to any tribal member who wanted to leave the reservation for work in the cities. Assistance came in the form of one-way paid transportation for the relocatee and his immediate family, plus a weekly allowance until he found a job and received his first paycheck. Assistance was also provided in locating housing, schools for the children, and other needs.

A vocational training component also was included. This part provided vocational training for any tribal member between eighteen and thirty-five years of age. The government paid a living allowance for the relocatee and his family, plus tuition costs for a period of up to two years.

It sounds like a good program, and it sounds even better when compared to the alternatives described by BIA field officer George Shubert in an article he wrote titled "Relocation News" for the *Fort Berthold Agency and New Bulletin* of Newton, North Dakota, on May 12, 1955. After painting a rosy urban picture of "skilled, lifetime jobs . . . with paid vacation, sick benefits, paid pension plan, union membership, etc.," Shubert writes:

> This office is presently equipped to offer financial assistance
> to a large number of qualified persons who have an earnest
> desire to improve their standard of living, by accepting
> permanent employment and relocation. . . . Our offices . . . are
> able to place on jobs and render any assistance necessary to

practically an unlimited number of families. . . . [A] good
selection of opportunities is available.

The rapidly rising waters in the bottom lands of the reservation should remind us of the fact that the Fort Berthold
people have lost forever . . . one-quarter of the area of the
entire reservation and one-half of the agricultural resources,
thereby rendering the reservation inadequate to provide
subsistence for the remaining members of the tribe.

We feel that a workable solution would be to avail yourselves of the opportunities offered by the Relocation Branch
of the BIA. It must be at least worthy of serious consideration
for persons who have ambitions to advance economically and
socially, and to provide better opportunities for their children.

The message provides a clear choice between no future on the
reservation and limitless bounty in the cities. But for the reader
who has doubts, a simpler, more brutal point is made in the closing statement: "If you won't do this much for yourself, at least do
it for the sake of your children."

One poster hanging in the Los Angeles Relocation Center in
1953 presents a scene that could have been taken right out of *Leave
It to Beaver*. The picture shows a sedate row of suburban tract
homes and inside are the smiling faces of Indian people proudly
showing off their perfect kitchens complete with garbage dispos-
als and brand-new television sets in ideal living rooms.

The tragic realities became all too clear to the new relocatee immediately upon arrival in the city. To begin with, the vocational
training program was inherently biased toward the lowest-status
careers. If an Indian wanted to become an auto mechanic or beau-
tician, the program paid tuition expenses plus a living stipend for
the trainee and his family. If, on the other hand, an Indian wanted
to attend college with ambitions for a white-collar career, the program paid only for the individual's expenses, not including the
family or tuition fees.

For those satisfied with blue-collar training, the living allowance
was provided only to relocatees who had no funds of their own.
Anyone found to have some resources, however limited, received
partial grants. The fine print betrays a harsh reality far different
from Shubert's grandiose claim of "any assistance necessary."

And although it may sound prudent to provide a stipend until

THE NEWS MEDIA: NEW START IN THE CITY.

The San Francisco News

SECOND SECTION   TUESDAY, JULY 24, 1956   Page 11

Editorials
Sports—Stocks
Want Ads

Meet The Big City Indians

6000 Due in Bay Area
By '57 Under U. S. Plans

In many a Bay Area city, you may encounter a coppery-hued man, with straight black hair and a stocky, muscular body. He belongs to that supposedly vanishing race — the American Indian. It's true, he is vanishing—from the reservation to the city relocation centers. And he's taking his place in the paleface world. Why is he leaving? How is he doing? This series gives the answers.—The Editor.

By William Steif

Louis Loretto is 45 and blind in one eye. He says:

"I'm standing in the middle and looking both ways."

With one eye, Louis Loretto sees more clearly than many of his fellow American Indians.

Loretto is a full-blooded Pueblo, from Jemez, N. M., and he has lived in San Francisco less than a year. With him in a five-room Candlestick Point apartment are his wife, Carrie, and seven children including grandchild.

One Son in the Navy

Another son is in the Navy and two older daughters are married and living in New Mexico.

What Loretto means by "looking both ways" is this: he liked reservation life—it was secure in tradition. But he knows he must press forward in the world-at-large for the sake of his children and, perhaps, even for his own self-respect.

Loretto is an electrician and an understanding, dignified man. He is probably better equipped than many Indians to face the world. But he is not unique. Thousands of Indians are detaching themselves from their reservation ties.

It is a difficult, often unhappy, task, but it may be part of the solution to what the U. S. calls its "Indian problem." The trouble with this solution is that it may kill the Indians' "Indian-ness."

Relocating Thousands

The U. S. Bureau of Indian Affairs, a branch of the Interior Department, is relocating thousands of Indians. Congress in 1953 resolved that the U. S. should prepare Indians to assume the same responsibilities as other citizens and turn Indian lands over to individuals or to private tribal corporations.

The bureau began a small-scale program of voluntary relocation in 1951. The congressional resolution accelerated this program and, as a result, some 10,000 Indians have moved to relocation centers in Chicago, Denver, Los Angeles or San Francisco-Oakland.

Since October, 1954, 1500 Indians have been brought to the Bay Area. By October, 1957, 3000 Indians will be here.

Why did the Lorettos leave?

"You don't want to leave the pueblo," says Mrs. Loretto, a short, chunky woman.

"But there were no jobs . . . we talked it over, sometimes I backed out, thinking of my little grandchildren, but finally we came here in August."

Bureau Found Him Job

A bureau representative took them to a hotel while a job for Loretto and housing for the family were found. The father went to work at Bethlehem Steel and the family moved into Ridgepoint Housing Project.

The train fare, a 3½-week subsistence allowance, housing and original job were all the bureau was obligated to furnish the Lorettos; actually it did considerably more.

It helped Loretto get a union card. It explained some of the workings of the big city and told him about the Inter-Tribal Friendship House in Oakland.

When Loretto was laid off in December, the BIA helped him find a new job.

But the Lorettos have helped themselves, too. In January they moved to Candlestick Point, which furnishes better living quarters for less money. Mrs. Loretto has been making pottery for sale. The family has been active in the local Indian organization, the Four Winds Club, and the Friendship House.

The success of the pottery has given Loretto an idea.

'We Like to Live Modern'

"My wife is an artist," he says, "maybe we have a little business, maybe have branches, one here and one at home, in Jemez." He adds:

"We've been to school (he went through high school; she through the 11th grade), we like to live modern, we like to have a little money to try to get started. . . .

"We like it here . . . we like it with the children intermixed at the public school, getting good education."

Then he looks the other way, and says:

"It is the hardest thing in the world to leave your own home on your own land . . . we had property, our own home.

"But there was not enough to make a living on . . . you plant just for yourself and it doesn't last all year, so you have to get a job. There's no rain, the water sometimes has to be rationed.

"You should be proud to keep on your traditions, teach your children."

Loretto pauses:

"People in cities always had the conception we got food from the government. Never in my life has the government come to my door. I always had to do it on my own."

Is there a plot to "steal" the Indians' remaining land?

"In my opinion," he answers, "there is not a plan to jeopardize anyone's property. There is hardly anything to steal now."

(Next: Debate and Delusions.)

Edna Loretto, seven, shows mother's pottery.

---

20 Sec. II—S.F. Examiner
Sunday, Sept. 29, 1957 ★ CCCC**

NEW INDIAN RELOCATION PLAN SUCCESS

Indians Migrate to S.F. for New Life

S.F. Examiner — 12/10/58

By LEWIS LAPHAM

The westward migration of many American Indians ends here in the Bay Area, but the hope of a

---

The San Francisco News

THIRD SECTION   THURSDAY, JULY 26, 1956   Page 19

Editorials
Sports—Stocks
Want Ads

Big City Indians

'Home Is the Reservation'

They Like Life in the City, But—

---

500 Indians Find Better Living Here

By BILL STOKES

Without fuss or fanfare, the Oakland Area has become the new reservation for some 500 Indians during the past year.

The human elements in a vast sociological experiment Uncle Sam is conducting, they have come to Oakland with their families from reservations throughout the country, gone to work and begun totally new lives in the strange and new environment of today's urban living.

That the program has been an unqualified success thus far is evidenced by the fact that the number of Indian residents in the "Oakland Area—will be trebled in the next 12 months.

This movement of Indians to the Oakland Area—and to Los Angeles, Chicago and Denver—is carried out under the three-year-old relocation program of the Bureau of Indian Affairs, a division of the U.S. Department of the Interior.

well in their jobs, and are making an average of about $1.76 an hour.

Indian trainees now are studying in such widely varying fields as plastics, barbering, ac-

HOUSING PROBLEM

"Homes still are a little diffi

showing amazing adeptness at their chosen vocations."

At the East Bay, yesterday opened an Indian Center in a two-story frame house at 2964 Telegraph Ave., with Miss Joan Adams as executive director.

NEW INDIAN CENTER—Present for the dedication of a new social center for Indians who have been relocated in the Oakland area are (front, from left) Mrs. Ethel Rogoff, center president; Miss Joan Adams, executive director; Mrs. Juanita Jackson, Mrs. Patsy Black and Mrs. Alice Carnes; and (rear) Morris Rogoff, Philip Jackson and William Black, secretary. The center is at 2964 Telegraph Ave.

the relocatee found permanent employment, the meaning of "permanent employment" was somewhat irrelevant for those unfortunate Indians who lost their jobs. Such was the case for many who found it impossible to work in a factory or a foundry after living all their lives on the reservation. The BIA allowed no margin for error on the part of the relocatee.

My own opinion of relocation, from the experiences of people I have known, is, like the historical record, ambivalent. Clearly, many policymakers saw in the program an opportunity to shirk the government's trust responsibility to the Indian at a lower long-term cost. Fewer reservation Indians meant reduced need for BIA services in the long run.

It is equally clear that the range of counseling services provided to the relocated family was appallingly inadequate. A bus ticket and a few weeks' allowance might be enough to get some settled anew in a city, but what about the young Indian family with limited English-language skills and virtually no comprehension of the madness of modern city life? Some Indian leaders believe the program hurt tribal government by draining off the supply of young, potential tribal leaders.

In defense of the program, it can be said that many relocatees eventually did find economic opportunity and a relatively higher standard of living. It is also true that many went back to the reservations to help their tribes with the skills they learned from the urban experience. As many Native Americans successfully adapted to urban ways, a new generation, a cadre of sophisticated, streetwise leaders emerged to promote our interests.

In 1974, the Menominee Restoration Act was passed owing to the significant efforts of Indian lawyers and activists. This historic legislation reversed the tide of federal termination policy that went hand in hand with relocation and signaled a new round in the fight for Indian rights.

Although Indians still suffer the highest school dropout and infant mortality rates, the lowest life expectancy and per capita incomes, and on and on, we are far from gone. We have not disappeared. We are no longer "the Vanishing American"—that popular romantic myth of the early 1900s. The 1990 census shows our numbers have increased about 90 percent since 1970—to more than one-and-a-half million—and more than two-thirds of us live in the cities.

Although some Indian people have been less fortunate, others have been able to adapt to the white man's world without abandoning the basic spiritual and traditional values of our people. In one of those cosmic ironies of sublime magnitude, the BIA's efforts to assimilate us have, in a word, backfired. By bringing together in the cities Indians from all tribes, relocation has contributed to pan-Indianism, the movement to smooth out individual tribal differences in favor of common goals. The great orators and chiefs of our past who counseled unity would have been proud.

> I know that my race must change. We cannot hold our own with the White man as we are. We only ask an even chance to live as other men live.
> —*Chief Joseph, Nez Percé*

On the evening of the last full moon of winter, the air was warm and alive with the smell of an early spring hanging thick like eucalyptus. High cirrus clouds made fire-red brush strokes across the cobalt blue sky, changing minute by minute the colors over San Francisco Bay. It was the kind of evening that always reminds me of the Navajo story "Born for the Sun," a story about First Man and First Woman, and about the birth of the hero Monster Slayer.

There is a place I like to go at times like this: a saddleback ridge running east to west in the Marin Headlands in the Bay Area, with a full, unbroken view in each of the four directions. On this particular night, all life seemed poised on the edge of the ancient promise.

A small bird dashed quietly by. A slow four-legged moved away in the tall grass. The wind was perfectly still. And finally, in glorious beauty it emerged, a giant, orange full moon, magic and surreal, slowly rising above the East Bay skyline.

The wind picked up and blew upon my face the sounds of the city below. It was the south wind. The People call it the Blue Wind, and it carried the sound of a million voices to my ears. Among those million voices, I heard many different tongues. Some were familiar to me and some were not. Others were unfamiliar to my ear, but in my heart, in another place long forgotten, I understood what they were saying.

They were the voices of Native America. Red men and women from a hundred different pueblos, forests, mesas, and prairies, coming together here, on this edge of the earth, to a green, wide dream of hills. To this land of Miwok and Ohlone, of Coyote and Falcon.

They were the voices of relocation. They are the fulfillment of the ancient promise: of spring, of the full moon, of the coming birth of the hero, and of life. Life that refuses to be legislated, relocated, or assimilated out of existence.

Memories of Growing Up in the Oakland Indian Community, circa 1952–66

Peggy Berryhill

You've asked me to comment on a photo taken the very day my family arrived in Oakland as part of the Relocation Program of the 1950s. I honestly don't recall much about the trip to California. We came by train, which for me it was all adventure. Looking at the photo, I see a five-year-old girl ready for anything, and my parents and brother and sister are tired and wondering about their future, our future in California.

I have some vague memories of our being sent to stay in a very small, one- or two-room apartment in some Victorian house near San Antonio Park. I believe it upset my parents that we were expected to live in such a cramped space. I don't remember the next

The Berryhill family in the relocation office on the day of their arrival in Oakland from Oklahoma in the 1950s. *Left to right:* Martha Berryhill, James Berryhill, Ronald Berryhill, Melissa Berryhill. *Front right:* Peggy Berryhill.

"home," but I do remember, fondly, the years we spent at High Street Homes housing project. We later moved to Alameda, where I finished grammar school and high school.

As I recall (remember, these are the memories of a time when I was under eight years old), there were several Indian families and many "Okies" who settled at the housing project. My mom walked to her job at the dry cleaners in Alameda. My dad drove to Crown Zellerbach Paper Company in San Leandro each day. (When I was eighteen, he died on the job site in San Leandro.) I've often joked that I'm an only child because my sister and brother, who are ten and eleven years older than I, left home by the time I was seven. As a result, I was raised as a "latch-key kid." After my parents made a few attempts at finding a good sitter for me, I ended up taking care of myself after school from the time I was about seven and a half. This is because my dad got home very soon after three in the afternoon. I shudder to think that in today's world my hard-working parents might be charged with neglect or endangerment because of this practice. Nevertheless, I survived without incident. I was and still am extremely self-sufficient, and being alone is not a problem for me.

I remember one of the first times I walked with my mother to the "corner store," which was in Alameda, just on the other side of the High Street Bridge. I had a harrowing and hilarious experience. As we were about halfway across the drawbridge, the alarm signal went off, and so did I! I ran until my mother finally caught me somewhere in Alameda on the other side of the bridge. After that incident, however, I always loved walking over the bridge, looking down at the water between the steel trestles, and watching the tugs and barges along the canal's narrow shore, and seeing small boats pass under when the bridge was raised. Often these walks ended at Lincoln Park, where I spent many happy hours, swinging, roller-skating, and playing croquet in the park's croquet court. Roaming the estuary was always a favorite pastime for kids from the project.

On weekends, we visited my aunt, uncle, and cousin in San Francisco. But, for many years, Intertribal Friendship House (IFH) was central to all my youth. Although we visited the first IFH, on Telegraph Avenue, only a few times that I recall, the subsequent IFH building near Laney College holds lots of memories of get-togethers. I recall Indian community dinners and, in particular, one celebration at the Oakland Auditorium. It was a Haskell reunion dinner when my dad was the oldest Haskell alumnus and

Bill Marin was the youngest. Bill's wife, Cece Marin, was one of the first directors of the current IFH. I think Billy Mills came to speak. There were long, decorated banquet tables, and our family cooked a lot of chicken, and other families brought other foods.

Big community meals have always been a part of the Indian community; we spent each Easter, Thanksgiving, Christmas with lots of families. I remember the Poolaws, Jacksons, Starrs, Sixkillers, Mankillers, and Davises, among others. Cakewalks were also a favorite event for the community. There were always Indian sports leagues, and I spent all my youth alternately playing softball or basketball. And going to church, always, Indian church. There was the IFH church on Sundays, with my Uncle Abe and my dad serving as lay preachers, and Walter Lasley, IFH icon, always attended. Once in a while we would have pancake breakfasts, and all the men would go out in the neighborhood and gather the local "hobos" and bring them in so they could eat. Today, these people would be the homeless.

There were also other churches. We Creeks had a store-front Methodist Church attended by about twelve families in San Francisco. This was on Shotwell and Eighteenth, I think. Each Sunday after church we would all share a meal together with food brought by all the families. There was also the Baptist Church in Visitation Valley, headed by George Smith. Everyone agreed the Choctaws were the best gospel singers. Also there was an Oakland Baptist Church where the Poolaws went. In East Oakland, the Eighth Avenue Methodist Church was a central place for many families for several years. My cousin and I were candle lighters for the service. I remember we loved the pomp and ceremony of it all, donning robes and walking somberly to the altar to light the candles. I think, however, we used to cut out after we played our part and traipse around the neighborhood until time to get back for the end of the service.

I also recall many picnics and Easter egg hunts in the Oakland Hills at Tilden Park above Ninety-eighth. My history with IFH waned after I graduated from high school and IFH moved to its present site. That IFH building at Seventh and Fallon Streets, the High Street Homes housing project, and my grammar school in Alameda are now gone. What remains is the legacy of a first-generation urban-raised person.

I have to credit the upbringing I had within the Indian community on both sides of the Bay—our sports, our picnics, and our good old *Indian*-Christian values—for who I am today. I was molded to be of service to our Indian communities. I have been given the opportunities to expand my life, and I can't second-guess what may or not have been possible had I grown up in Oklahoma. I have to believe that growing up in California made a profound difference in my life. I acquired many skills that helped my personal development en route to becoming the premiere radio documentarian among Indians.

Peggy Berryhill, 2000.

When I look at the picture of the five-year-old girl eager for adventure, I see that I have never lost that zeal. Learning to take risks, learning to let go of self-imposed fears, and having a willingness to *learn* every day of life are also lessons I incorporated from parents, family, and community. Other "city" skills include learning to relate to a diverse population, learning to "go between worlds" (Indian and non-Indian) without developing schizophrenia, and maintaining pride in my heritage with the dignity that my parents instilled in me.

In my career as a journalist, I often ask (Indian) people who are walking new paths, "What made the difference for you?" I ask this because in my travels throughout Indian country I see too many of our current youth languishing in passivity or trapped by fears, sometimes with disastrous results—rage turned inward resulting in death through alcohol or drugs, or feelings of hopelessness turned outward with equally negative results. All I know is that the paths that led me to be who I am now were not easy to follow and were often fraught with fears and trepidation. I had my share of years of drifting, without purpose. But because of these experiences I eventually became the person I am now and feel comfortable with the life I have earned after facing up to all the barriers of poverty, racism, and all the "isms" that hover around anyone growing up in the city. What made the difference, I wonder, for me and for all the others? A clue might be found in the face of the five-year-old facing adventure and fear head-on.

"That's why I suggested that name because there were a lot of tribes beginning to come in at that time. So when the council and the board members wanted to know what we should name the House, I suggested 'Intertribal.' And they accepted it. And the other part, 'Friendship.' We had to find that word someplace and put it there. They finally decided on 'Friendship,' so we voted on it, and it became Intertribal Friendship House."

—*Ethel Rogoff*

On the steps of the first Intertribal Friendship House on Telegraph Avenue, about 1956. Ethel Rogoff is in the striped blouse.

"It wasn't an easy life for me, even after I came to Oakland because everything was different."
—*Alice Carnes*

"If there was no Friendship House, I would have gone home ten times over, I was so lonely."
—*Irmlee Yellow Eagle*

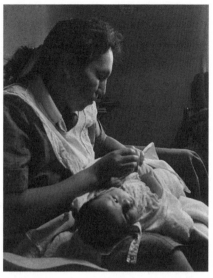

Irmlee Yellow Eagle and her baby, about 1958.

"That is me when I was a baby on my mom's lap in the photo. We left Oakland after about three years and moved to the reservation back home for a year. Then we went to Cleveland, Ohio, through relocation again. She was one of the people who founded the Cleveland American Indian Center. We stayed there ten years and then returned to Rosebud. She eventually finished her B.A. degree in human services when she was in her fifties. Altogether she had seven children, and I'm sixth in line. For many years, she was an advocate and sat on the board of the White Buffalo Calf Women's Shelter, a domestic violence–prevention shelter for women here. In February of 2000, she passed on. She always pushed me to be active in the tribe and I think would be proud of me now. I was just installed last week as vice-chair of our tribe."
—*Glen Yellow Eagle, Irmlee's son, Mission, South Dakota*

Quiet Desperation

Floyd Red Crow Westerman and Jimmy Curtiss

My soul is in the mountains, my heart is in the land,
But I'm lost here in the city; there's so much I don't understand.
And the quiet desperation coming over me, coming over me.
I gotta leave, I can't stay another day.
There's an emptiness inside of me.
I can't bear the loneliness out here;
There's another place I gotta be . . .
(hums repeat) Another place I gotta be.

I long for you Dakota, smell the sweetgrass on the plain;
I've seen too much meanness, and I feel too much pain,
And this quiet desperation coming over me, coming over me.
I gotta leave, I can't stay another day.
There's an emptiness inside of me.
I can't bear the loneliness out here;
There's another place I gotta be . . .
(hums repeat) Another place I gotta be.

Hungry Eyes in the Wind

Alisha Russell

Mother Earth
I hear your cry
in the winds
among the city
sounds
overflowed with
people searching,
in need of love
or a caring hand
maybe just a smile
or hello

A Winter Day

My Dad turned on a lamp
to read the paper.
My family are Indians.
The cat went to bed in his kitty box.
It was a rainy day in winter.
I was thinking of the waves of the ocean
going over my head.
I was drinking chocolate milk
And remembering my grandmother
in Oklahoma.

—*George, Heather, Estella, and Manuel*

The Uprooted Indians-- Dead End in Bay Area

'Just Too Much'

Harassed Indian Woman Gives Up, Departs Oakland

Alameda Times-Star 5/29/68

It just got to be too much for Stella Leach.

The Oakland nurse, whose Sioux ancestry caused her and her six children to be targets of constant harassment by other residents of their neighborhood, has packed up and moved to San Leandro.

Mrs. Leach is staying with another Indian woman in San Leandro and her children are temporarily in a motel. She said she hopes to find a home for all of them by the first of the month.

The Leach family's troubles began shortly after she rented a modest, two-bedroom home at 3112 Kingsland St. in Oakland. The neighbors, resentful of her Indian lineage, began making threats, including obscene telephone calls and messages scrawled on the house walls.

When that didn't rout the "intruders," the front door was ripped off its hinges, the family possessions were ransacked, and many acts of violence were committed, she told authorities.

That was when she declared she was "sick of moving once a year," and would fight for her home.

But the women in her neighborhood started screaming at her "like fishwives," she said, and she started to pack.

"It just got to be too much," she sighed.

The all-day packing job was done with the help of an estimated 250 persons — Mexican-Americans, white students from the University of California, and Mills College, Negroes, and "a few Jewish ladies who had escaped from Hitler."

Released Poverty Funds

Indian Protesters Victorious

The California Weekly **People** SAN FRANCISCO EXAMINER
SUNDAY, SEPTEMBER 29, 1968

San Francisco's Troubled Indians

The plight of urban Indians

By Neal R. Peirce

MINNEAPOLIS — If you embrace all of Ronald Reagan's and Dave Stockman's budget cuts as a proper purgative for bloated government spending, then come to poverty-ridden, garbage-strewn Franklin Avenue in south Minneapolis.

Here, in a neighborhood of 22,000 people that belies the Twin Cities' clean, progressive image, is the largest agglomeration of Indians in any American city. Deep trouble has accompanied the urban migration of these native peoples — there is an array of social pathologies: massive unemployment, alcoholism, vagrancy, knifings, rapes and chronic welfare dependency.

Doorways are littered with broken glass. People live in abandoned cars during Minnesota's winters.

But, go inside Branch One, a Catholic charities' drop-in center where some 300 Indians come each day for a cup of coffee or a sandwich, and you discover an unusual scene. It is the office of the American Indian Business Development Corporation (AIBDC) — the only organization devoted to economic development for city Indians in all America.

Brenda Draves, 32, a part-Indian from Wisconsin, heads AIBDC. The board president is Charlotte White. This little group believes urban Indians can turn a new leaf and that Indian-owned, Indian-manned business enterprises are the way to start.

But urban Indians are poor. For seed capital, AIBDC has sought heavy government subsi-

dy to mount the enterprise Draves and her crew believe could be a ticket to future self-sufficiency — a proposed two-block shopping center at the heart of Franklin Avenue, just 13 blocks from downtown Minneapolis.

That $2.6 million shopping center, four years in the planning, was on a fast track toward ground-breaking when Reagan became president. Architects' drawings were complete; the city had assembled land from 20 private owners. Two "class A" tenants, including a supermarket, had been recruited. The Northwestern National Life Insurance Company had agreed to a $750,000 loan. A federal Urban Development Action Grant (UDAG) for $550,000 was committed.

But there was a vital, missing ingredient: a $1.3 million shopping center construction grant from the Economic Development Administration (EDA). No one had been more supportive of the Indians' effort than the EDA. The agency urged them to proceed at every step, assured them early final approval of the loan. But in the fall, there was a bureaucratic snafu at EDA, delaying the final sign-off. January 20 came, Reagan took office, and still there were no final papers. And then the new administration froze the EDA's grant-making power.

The result: despair on Franklin Avenue, indeed a deep feeling of betrayal by the federal government. AIBDC has been desperately trying to persuade the Reaganites to relent and let the Franklin Avenue grant be consummated.

The Franklin Avenue issue raises disturbing questions. Will the nation again add to its long list of broken promises to its native peoples? Is Dave Stockman, in disparaging EDA and all government subsidies for business in depressed areas, selling valid economic theory — or economic snake oil?

"EDA doesn't create jobs; it (simply) reallocates them," the OMB director would have us believe. EDA and UDAG grants "impose an economic cost on the overall economic efficiency of the private sector."

The idea that targeted government investment here would be wasteful is hard to accept. There are a dozen local businesses that have promised to invest $100,000 to $600,000 each on nearby streets, and hire many more Indians, if the shopping center is built.

City official Jim White notes that "public investment around Franklin Avenue has been enormous" — several high rises for the elderly, a new library, a Native American Center for Indian exhibits and social services, repaved streets, a new junior high school. "But the neighborhood is still garbage because we're missing the economic development function," White says. "You can put public money down all sorts of rat holes, but unless you have private people willing to put in dough as well, the neighborhood can't be viable again."

Neal R. Peirce writes for the National Journal.

The Indian's Struggle to Live

- San Francisco lures them ... almost half return home
- Any Indian can move free ... they want restrictions
- They get support money ... they want part-time jobs

"Well, the only thing was I didn't have any friends, you know. I was brought up in boarding school. I was used to all kinds of friends then. I really missed it when I first came. I used to lie in bed and cry sometimes because I was so lonely. I was actually lost in the city. I was all alone. So were these people from the reservations, especially direct from the reservations. I know they find it lonely. My mother had the same experience. She was lonely, so that's the reason why we used to return home now and then. So, I can't describe—Any of you ever been lonesome? I mean, it's the funniest thing, no matter how people are good to you and do things, nice things, for you, you still can't ever cure that lonely feeling."

—*Ethel Rogoff*

Little one at the beach, about 1960.

Goin' Back

Floyd Red Crow Westerman

Goin' back, to where the land I love,
Goin' back, to where the truth began,

Back to the land I left behind,
Back to the pride that I must find;

Leave me alone,
Can't you see I'm goin' home.

Goin' back, to where I'm gonna stay,
Goin' back, to try an' find the way,
Back to the land I left behind,
Back to the pride that I must find;

Leave me alone,
Can't you see I'm goin' home.

Back to the mountains and the prairie,
Back to the desert and the hills,
Catch up to the buffalo,
And where the rivers flow

Goin' back and there I'm gonna stay,
Goin' back to try and find the way,
Back to the land I left behind,
Back to the pride that I must find,

Leave me alone,
Can't you see I'm goin' home.
Can't you see I'm goin' home.

San Francisco

The ocean breeze in big waves
French bread
Fish, lobsters, and crabs
Cars running fast
A roller coaster going up and down.

—*Aggie Aranaydo, Hintil Kuu Ca School*

My Relocation Experience

Yvonne Lamore-Choate (Quechan)

In May 1969, I came to the San Francisco Bay Area through the Bureau of Indian Affairs (BIA) Relocation Program. My parents and I had been through the Relocation Program before, moving to Denver, Colorado, in 1960 from the Ft. Yuma Indian reservation. After my mother passed away and my father remarried, I decided it was time to venture out on my own at the age of twenty-three.

However, nothing prepared me for my first impression of Oakland. If you've ever been to the Oakland Greyhound bus depot, you know what I mean. Later, I discovered Oakland was not such a bad town; you just had to know what areas to stay out of. With all my worldly possessions in tow, I took a cab to the Tourraine Hotel. The cab driver reeked of alcohol, and I later found out that although the Tourraine was only about five blocks from the bus depot, the driver had taken me on a tour of Oakland in order to get a larger fare. Thus, my indoctrination into the real world had begun.

That first day in the hotel room, I sat and wondered whatever possessed me to choose such a place, where I knew absolutely no one. The small hotel room only added to my despair. The room smelled musty and stale from years of cigarette smoke and the faint scent of Pine-Sol. There was a single lightbulb hanging from the ceiling by a long electrical wire. The bed was one of those old cast-iron beds with a lumpy mattress, and the dreaded communal bathroom! I sat there and cried, feeling sorry for myself and feeling so alone.

The next day was a little better. I found my way to the BIA office in Alameda to attend classes for the new relocatees. In these classes, we were instructed on how much of a stipend we would get each month, what other assistance the BIA would give us, like a clothing allowance, and how to use the transit system. The group I was in was made up mostly of single women who were either going to attend some kind of business school or cosmetology school. It was fun getting to know each other, but by the end of the week we would all scatter to different parts of the Bay Area: some would remain in Oakland, others would go to San Jose or Hayward, and some of us to San Francisco. Our paths would cross again over the years at one Indian bar or another. In the 1960s, there were Indian bars everywhere, and they all seemed to be doing a very lucrative business.

I ended up going to San Francisco and rooming at a residence club. These residence clubs were pretty common around that time, catering to young, single people and providing some semblance of family. My roommate was a young Mojave girl from Parker, Arizona. We soon discovered that we were distantly related and knew some of the same people. I am an enrolled member of the Quechan tribe, and my Indian heritage also includes Mojave and Maricopa.

Life settled into a routine of classes and the wonders of learning new things every day. I was like a sponge absorbing everything around me: the different foods, sights such as Fisherman's Wharf, Chinatown, and Golden Gate Park. My absolute favorite was to take the bus all the way out to Land's End and to the old Playland Amusement Park. Because I was living on a limited income, it was an inexpensive way to get entertainment and a meal of hot dogs on a lonely weekend. I would sit for hours watching people and enjoying the sunset.

The Bay Area seemed to be a mecca for Indians around that time, and with the occupation of Alcatraz in 1969 more Indians were arriving every day. It was estimated that there were around twenty thousand Indians in the Bay Area at that time. There was a radio program about Alcatraz that I listened to every night. I envied those going out and wished I had the courage to go out and take part in the history-making events. However, I didn't want to jeopardize my chance to get an education and be able to support myself.

About nine months into my training, my counselor at the BIA told me that there was a job opening for a secretary at the Native American studies office at UC Berkeley. He felt that I would have a good chance at the position and arranged for me to have an interview.

The next day I arrived at the Native American studies office and was greeted by two friendly students, a Tohono O'odham (called Papago in those days) girl from Sells, Arizona, and a young man from the Cheyenne River Sioux tribe. Lee Brightman was the coordinator of Native American studies, a very charismatic man and somewhat intimidating. He stood about six foot three or four, with huge muscles and a crew cut, left over from his days as a marine. Lee told me that his secretary had left her job to take part in the occupation at Alcatraz. He didn't know if she would be back, but he needed someone in the office because the 1970 spring semester was about to begin.

We went into Lee's office, and after some idle chitchat he began to dictate a letter to me. He wanted to write a letter to one of the original American Indian Movement (AIM) founders and started dictating his letter: "Dear . . . , you goddamned mother f——!" I stopped dictation and looked up at Lee, wondering if I'd heard him correctly. He asked, "What's the matter?" I said, "They never taught us how to write such words in shorthand!" He just busted out laughing and toned down his letter a bit. Later I would learn that this was the way Lee spoke; these words were nothing out of the ordinary, and he meant no harm by them.

After the interview, Lee told me he had two other people to interview and that he'd contact the BIA and let them know his decision. I went to class the next day, and around 10:00 A.M. my counselor from BIA called and told me I got the job and to report to work that same day. I left Munson Business School that day and never returned. It was like a dream; one day I'm in school and the next I'm working at one of the most prestigious universities in the country, in one of the first Native American studies programs in the nation.

While working at the Native American studies office, I came to know some of the people who were the major forces in the Alcatraz occupation. I got involved with coordinating donations of food

Relocated young women at boardinghouse dinner, early 1960s.

and clothing to Alcatraz, and I tried to help in any way I could—for example, typing papers for some of the students who were living on the island. Some students and faculty from those early Native American studies days have risen to prominence in the Indian world. On occasions when I run into them, I sense an uneasiness in them that I may remind them of their wilder, more carefree days at Berkeley and maybe the fear that I might share this knowledge with others. No need to worry, I'm not writing an exposé, yet! There are also former students and faculty who have remained the same all these years. When I run into them, it's always such a good feeling. My oldest and dearest friend, Susan (Hannan) Tsosie, and I joke with each other that because we've been friends for more than thirty years, we can't afford to become enemies; we have too much dirt on each other! My years at the Native American studies office were very exciting and rewarding—I couldn't have dreamed up a more exciting job! It's that old adage of being at the right place at the right time.

Relocatees' secretarial job training, early 1960s.

These days, when Susan and I run into Lee Brightman at pow-wows or at our local donut shop, he'll say, "God, you guys are old!" We then proceed to remind him that if he thinks we're old, how old does that make him? He just laughs. He is one person who has remained the same over the years: honest and forthright and a genuinely good person. I have the upmost respect for Lee and am grateful for the opportunity to have worked for him.

Through the years, I've worked for some great Indian programs, such as the American Indian Higher Education Consortium and the American Indian Education Program of the Oakland Public Schools. Although the relocation experience didn't work out for many people, it gave me a chance to experience some wonderful things in my life!

Singles Supper Club at Intertribal Friendship House, 1959. Left side, front to back: Leo Mike, Betty Frank, Sandy Davidson, Sandy Weaver, Sandy Romero, ——, ——. Right side, front to back: Freddie Yazzie, Jonny Smith, Denny Stanley, Lee ——, Helen Stanley, Sarah Poncho, ——, Joan Adams.

"The Singles Supper Club met on Wednesday evenings. They paid fifty cents for supper. There were usually forty or forty-five young people. I don't know how we ever squashed them around the tables. I remember card tables stretched from one end of the House to the other, with chairs just jammed along the sides. But, really, I think it was a dating bureau."

—*Joan Adams*

"I didn't get paid because I was a volunteer. Every Wednesday night I would go down there and feed a lot of young people. We had a nice program going on. Now all these young people that I used to work with all met together and got married and have their families now."

—*Alice Carnes*

"After I left Intertribal House, and I had returned home to Kelowna [in Canada], I was asked to be the director of the first Canadian Indian center. This was called the Winnipeg Indian and Metis Friendship Center. It's interesting that they picked up the name 'Friendship' from the Oakland center, and that later, every Indian center across Canada—well, almost every Indian center—was called a 'Friendship Center.'"

—*Joan Adams*

"And there weren't too many people who had cars. So whoever had cars, we'd all rush over and pile in and sit on top of each other. We'd have our own pow-wows up in the hills. We had car lights on in the night, dancing around in the dirt. Oh, Lord, we'd be dirty by the time we got out. Somebody always managed to have a drum. There was always somebody who knew how to sing, too."

—*Joyce Keoke and Madge Goodiron Jones*

Lucy Hale, Ruth Pachert, and Mary Watson, three sisters in the city, about 1955.

"There were three of us that moved into an apartment down by Lake Merritt. We stayed together like little baby chicks, all in a cluster. Somebody mapped out a route for me from Oakland to the San Francisco terminal, and I just followed that little route faithfully every day. I didn't look from one side to the other or across the street. Oh, I was really scared. I don't know; it's such a big city, you could just get swallowed up if you wandered away from where you knew you were going. I did that for about six months because it seemed so huge, and I didn't know anybody there, and nobody knew me. If I got swallowed up, nobody would even miss me for months. I was afraid. It was kind of a frightening feeling. And you know, those bus drivers, some of them would just holler at you. I was frightened of the whole thing."
—*Millie Ketcheshawno*

The Three Sisters—Daughters of Mary Watson, January 11, 2001

Marlene Watson

The three sisters in the photo—Marlene Watson, Laura Davis, and Bonnie Williams—are Navajo: Bonnie is the eldest at forty-five years old, Laura is forty-one, and Marlene is the youngest at thirty-nine years old. All were born in Oakland and currently reside in Oakland. Bonnie is presently attending Laney College in Oakland. She will receive her two-year certificate in the culinary arts program in June 2001. Her goal is to attend the California Academy of Arts and pursue a career in culinary arts as a master chef. She attended a literacy program a year and a half ago and has exceeded all expectations in her studies and leadership skills.

Bonnie and Laura have learned the cooking skills of their mother, Mary Watson. They learned to make delicious fry bread, chili beans, and beef stew. Mary Watson and her husband Bennie Watson were involved in community meetings and events in the 1950s and 1960s in Oakland. The family has followed their parents' example of leadership in participating in American Indian community events. The Watson family had food booths at pow-wows, and the children learned how to cook, to practice entrepreneurial skills, and to work hard.

Laura Davis has five children and one grandson. She has operated her own 23-Hour Watch Day Care and Foster Care in Oakland, and her husband, Timothy Davis, and family presently own and manage a family music ministry, Lamb's Bride Production. Laura and family have attended Evangelical Outreach Church for eighteen years, and she has participated in American Indian programs with her children, while also volunteering in fund-raising events.

Marlene has received her master's degree in civil engineering and architectural design from the University of California, Berke-

Left to right: Marlene Watson, Laura Davis, and Bonnie Williams, daughters of Mary Watson, 2000.

ley. She works as a design manager for Bovis Lend Lease, a project management firm that oversees new construction of public schools in Oakland. Marlene has taught martial arts classes and encourages young American Indian students to pursue a career in the sciences.

Marlene and Bonnie have attended Victory Outreach Church in Oakland for the past four years. The photo was taken at the Victory Outreach Fifteenth-Year Anniversary Celebration on November 5, 2000. The Lord has blessed us with a loving and caring mother who stressed getting an education and helping others.

"We lived over on Vermont, off Grand, up on the hill over there. We had an old Nash with a bad transmission. It couldn't make it up in the front gears, so my stepdaddy, he used to back the Nash up the hill."

—*Bill Wahpepah*

Christmas girl, Bill and Bessie Leno's granddaughter, Audrey, at Intertribal Friendship House on Telegraph Avenue, about 1957.

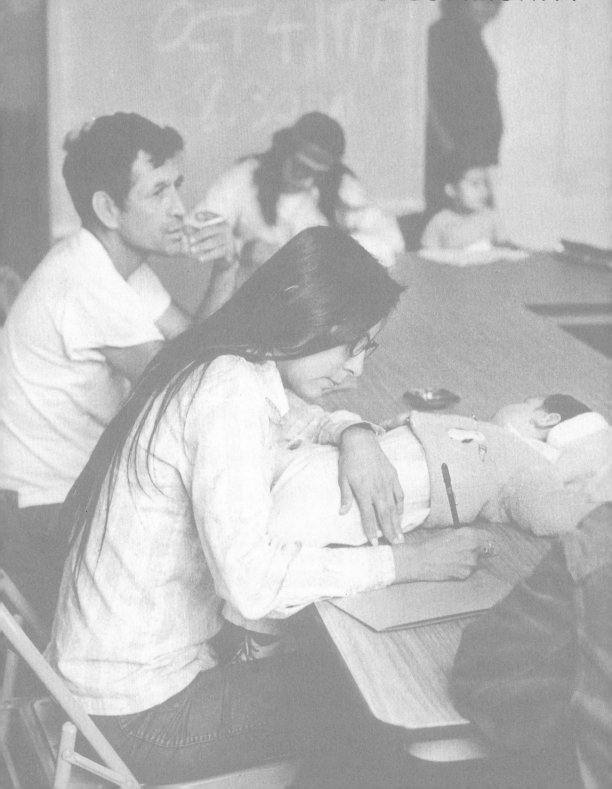

PART THREE BUILDING COMMUNITY

One of the instrumental organizations in the Bay Area Indian community has been Intertribal Friendship House (IFH), founded in 1955. As one of the first Indian-focused, multipurpose urban organizations in the United States, it became a stimulus and to some extent an informal model for similar urban Indian centers in cities throughout the United States and Canada. A variety of social services and cultural and recreational programs and activities have been offered at IFH since its inception, including summer youth programs, educational activities, Elders programs, holiday dinners, social service counseling, and a gift shop. The facilities also serve as a community meeting hall and conference center, and families gather here for receptions, memorials, and other family events.

As the Indian community grew in numbers, it also diversified in terms of tribal representation, age, and occupations. This diversity has been reflected in the development of specialized organizations that address specific needs. With the number of American Indians in the Bay Area increasing during the 1960s and 1970s, the proliferation and diversification of these organizations continued and has included among others the Native American Health Center with facilities in San Francisco and Oakland, the American Indian Child Resource Center, United Indian Nations, the Indigenous Nations Child and Family Agency, the San Francisco Indian Center, the San Jose Indian Center, the American Indian Family Healing Center, the Friendship House Association of American Indians, the International Indian Treaty Council, the American Indian Baptist Church, Hintil Kuu Ca, American Indian Contemporary Arts, California Indian Legal Services, the American Indian Public Charter School, the American Indian Film Institute, and the American Indian AIDS Institute of San Francisco. Many others have come and gone.

These organizations are focal points of pride and power in the Indian community and bring people of all tribes together in working for community well-being. From the loneliness and isolation of the few individuals who migrated to the Bay Area in the 1930s and 1940s, a large and vigorous American Indian community has emerged.

INTERTRIBAL
FRIENDSHIP HOUSE

AMERICAN INDIAN
CENTER

1984

1984 calendar cover illustration.

Bay Area Princesses. Pow-wow at Stern Grove, San Francisco, 1956. *Left to right:* Billie June Davis, Clara Davis, ———, Charlene Jacobson, Coleen Howell, Millie Ketcheshawno, Betty Hayes Frank, Lydia Sanchez.

"I was asked to run for Bay Area Princess. I didn't have any Navajo outfit, so I tried my best to explain it to my foster parents. She made me a Navajo skirt. I showed her. I didn't have any jewelry, so we had to run around all over to get jewelry and get me moccasins, too. I was the first runner-up. I was sponsored by Friendship House. This was the first pow-wow in the area."

—*Helen Stanley*

Millie Ketcheshawno in November 1999 at the thirtieth anniversary of the occupation of Alcatraz: "documentarian, film producer, and participant on Alcatraz 1969–71; freedom, sovereignty, dignity, and most of all for your laughter" —John Whitefox.

"In 1956, that was the only pow-wow we had in the Bay Area in those days. It was on Labor Day in Stern Grove in San Francisco. Pow-wows didn't flow like they do today; there was not continuous singing and dancing. The singers we had, had to have a break. It was new to all of us. Paul Moya was one of the singers. He was from the Southwest. I went to Haskell with him. Pow-wows were new to us, and that was one of the things that glued us together. We were always looking forward to it. Then, in the '60s, we started to have more, and we got together and ate, talked, and danced."

—*Millie Ketcheshawno*

51

"And then all the food they had! They used to have chili beans, fry bread. Everybody wanted fry bread, at least once a month or so. So they would have the fry bread at the Friendship House, and that's when the women who know how to make it would make it."
—*Joyce Keoke and Madge Goodiron Jones*

Sarah Poncho's Fry Bread Recipe

Mix four cups of all-purpose flour and two tablespoons of baking powder. Add one teaspoon of salt. Then take one cup of half warm milk and half warm water, and add it slowly as you go, mixing it with the flour. Work it through and then work it more until it is mixed and you can work with it. Make it into small balls about the size of golf balls. Then roll it out and cook it in about one-quarter inch of hot vegetable oil. When it is bubbly and golden color, turn it over. Then take it out and let the oil drip off; put it on a paper towel and eat it! That's the way. Now you try it.

Wednesday Night Dinner at Intertribal Friendship House, 1967. *Facing the camera, left to right:* Alice Carnes, Pauline Hickman, Minnie Ellen Hastings, Bessie Leno, Mrs. Brown.

The Community Mental Health Training Program

Gerri Martinez Lira, M.S.W.

I was very fortunate to have come to the Bay Area during the times of change (1950s, 1960s, and 1970s) that included the postwar years, the war on poverty, and the self-determination movement. Intertribal Friendship House (IFH) was the Indian Center, where everyone went to meet other Indian people and to socialize. There were many who had problems, and it soon became apparent that there was a need for a social worker. Carol Baxter, M.S.W., was the third social worker hired at IFH in the 1960s. She was successful in working with families and individuals and was able to identify issues including health care, poverty, and alcoholism, as well as other culture-related issues that needed addressing by Indian people.

Carol knew there had to be a way to solve these problems, so during 1970–71 she wrote and received a grant from the National Institute of Mental Health to train American Indians as community mental health workers and advocates. The focus was on American Indians helping and working in their own community and was funded to train ten American Indians at the associate's degree (A.A.) level. Classes were held at IFH and Merritt College, a local community college. Carol taught and supervised the students in case management, advocacy, and group-identified cultural issues.

This program was very successful, and the students received an A.A. degree in community mental health. It was funded twice, in 1971–73 and 1973–75, by the National Institute of Mental Health and was a model program that became a catalyst for similar American Indian community programs throughout the United States. I was a participant in both programs. Many of the participants continued their education, receiving B.A. and M.A. degrees. They continued to work in the Bay Area Indian community, creating new programs and serving as directors, supervisors, and social workers. Others went back to their reservations to become social workers, judges, and child advocates. Some of these students became known on a national level in their field.

Carol Baxter resigned her position at IFH at the end of the training program. She felt her work was completed. She went on to

Board meeting at Intertribal Friendship House, about 1970. *Left to right:* Ray Billy, ——, Juanita Jackson, ——, Mrs. Leno, ——, Walter Lasley, Bill Leno.

work for Peralta College and taught at Merritt College until she retired in 2000. She remains in Oakland. We are very honored to have known Carol, who through her devotion and support to American Indians in the Bay area taught us skills to strengthen our community. She continues to be a good friend to all of us.

"We have almost 100 percent at all of the meetings. I mean, the majority. They say, 'How do you do that?' and I say, 'During the elections, you choose all your friends and make sure they get elected.' They say, 'Is that legal?' And I say, 'Well, they're parents.' They say, 'That's true.' I say, 'The next thing is, don't have long drawn-out meetings. You can do a lot as a board member. As an employee you can do a lot, but I think that as a board member, a lot of the big decisions are made.'"

—*Justine Buckskin*

"We decided we should have a trading post because a lot of women did beadwork and other things, and we had no outlet for it. We thought if we had a trading post, we could give people a chance to buy it."

—*Juanita Jackson*

"It's usually all women that are on the boards and come to meetings. Men are busy with their jobs, or they're on their union boards or whatever. We have a hard time convincing them that the Indian community is just as important. Any man who ran for a board seat probably got it just because we wanted the male perspective."
—*Rosalie McKay-Want*

Walter Lasley: A Memorial

Wes Huss

Walter Lasley was an exceptional person who played an important role in the development of the Bay Area Indian community and in my life. Walter was a Potowatami, born on the Sac and Fox Reservation in Kansas in 1896, who had lived and worked in Oakland for many years before finding a place in the leadership at Intertribal Friendship House (IFH). His first visit to IFH was on May 21, 1957. I know that date very well because it was also my first day there. He and I kept asking each other questions about the House and wondering why the other wouldn't give straight answers. Then, suddenly, we each realized that we both were new, and we had the first of many good laughs together.

Shortly after Walter started to come to the House, he became a member of the IFH Indian Council, which planned all the programs. Later he was elected to the board of directors and served on it from then on.

Recently I had a chance to talk with Darrell Standing Elk and check out some of my memories of Walter. Darrell, who came to the Bay Area from the Rosebud reservation in South Dakota in 1958, was also a close friend of Walter. He spoke of how important Walter was to him, especially during those first years when he was lonely. Walter was like an uncle—teasing and giving encouragement, bolstering, by his example, Darrell's resolve to stay here.

In 1958, when IFH moved from its first location—the small residential structure at Twenty-ninth and Telegraph—to the larger building at 51 Ninth Street, Walter moved in as resident director in charge of overseeing the young men who rented rooms there. Darrell, who lived there for several years, said that Walter was a perfect man for the House. Whatever difficulty the young men might have with each other or with others, they would try to keep from bringing it into the House out of respect for him.

One of the ways that Walter helped build the sense of community among Indian people was to attend Indian events all over the Bay Area. He'd get into his 1950 Pontiac, with either himself or Darrell driving, and take off at a moment's notice. He never missed a pow-wow in spite of the pain that he often had because of his arthritis. He would just take some more Bufferin and be on his way.

Walter had been a taxi driver for many years before having to retire because of his legs. He told Darrell that the many years of sitting and driving the taxi had caused his legs to bow out. But, characteristically, he used to joke even about that. He liked to tell about the young boy who said to him: "Gee, Walter, you must have done a lot of horseback riding."

He was a formidable domino player. I never saw him lose a game. He was no longer a betting man when he started at IFH. If he had been, he could have cleaned out most of Oakland or, at any rate, anybody foolhardy enough to sit down and play with him.

Walter Lasley.

He enjoyed associating with younger people, and he believed in perpetuating traditions. For example, when young Henry St.John, who had danced back home on the reservation, came to the city, Walter found out that Henry needed a costume and sponsored his coming out with a giveaway. Henry remembers that as happening about 1964. I believe that was the first such ceremony held in the Bay Area.

Walter was always eager to talk to other Indian people about their ideas and ways. He was among the group that started to get together at IFH in the late 1950s to discuss Indian concerns. They carried on an investigation of the relocation office and its practices, and made recommendations, some of which were accepted. Later the group became the United Bay Area Council on American Indian Affairs.

In 1961, Walter went to the nationwide American Indian conference held at the University of Chicago and came back with renewed vigor and dedication to build a sense of community and to work on Indian issues.

Prior to that, in 1958, Frank Quinn, who was then the American Friends Service Committee field-worker and who had been visiting the Indian prisoners in San Quentin, asked me if I knew anyone in the Indian community who might be interested in taking on the responsibility for a monthly visit. I immediately thought of Walter, who said, "Sure," without a moment's hesitation. He kept up those visits to San Quentin from then on once a month until the end. He started to take Indian visitors with him and made arrangements for dancers, singers, and others to attend a yearly pow-wow. Some of those he involved in the visits continued to make the visits after he passed away.

I'd like to quote from the *San Quentin Prison American Indian Cultural Group Newsletter* (1969), words written about Walter shortly after his death:

> Mr. Walter Lasley, long known to his people as a great humanitarian and to the Indian convicts of San Quentin as their leader, died peacefully after a short illness on Sunday morning, May 4, 1969. He was 73.
>
> . . . In the past 11 years Walter rarely missed a monthly meeting with the Indian men of San Quentin. In recent years he suffered from crippling arthritis, yet continued coming to our meetings, often in a wheelchair.
>
> . . . He was indeed the driving force in encouraging the Indian community to participate in the program here and was instrumental in overseeing that the Indian convicts have a representative voice in the free world. His wisdom, guidance and enthusiasm was the "backbone" for the American Indian Cultural Group.
>
> . . . His advice was simple, wise and softly spoken. He always emphasized that the Indian People must speak out and express themselves. He did not try to lecture or condemn, preach or cure-all; he simply listened with a deep understanding of a lifetime knowledge of his people and then spoke of the Indian ways.
>
> . . . He advocated unity among all Indians, and moreover, he was a perfect example of a true and understanding human being.
>
> . . . This man led a good, full and constructive life. Now that he is gone, the strength of his broad grin—his trademark for encouragement—will be missed, but he will always remain highly respected and remembered.

In closing, let me say that I realize that this short memorial doesn't do justice to this fine man, Walter Lasley.

Hooty.

Doug.

Letter to brothers and sisters, 1982

Patrick E. Croy Sr. [Hooty Croy]
P.O. Box C-07501
Tamal, Calif. 94974
April 13, '82

Brothers & Sisters

Greetings. I received the calendar and poster and I send special thanks. Life on death row is very depressing, but the Brothers on the row stand as one in our struggle. They try to keep us separated but they can't suppress the unity in our heart.

The Brothers on the row have little communication from the free world but our strength in prayer is with you and for your struggles.

My father perform at the annual music festival (Charlie Thom) and later stopped to visit. It was good to see him.

The only religious freedom I'm allowed is within, where I thank the great spirit I was borned Indian.

In total resistance of this slow death.
Patrick Croy, Douglas Stankewitz

Pow-wow planning meeting, 1977. *Seated, front to back:* Jo Helen Nunes with daughter Kimberly Casey Nunes, Carl Sands, ——, ——. *Standing:* Carl's son, Sammy Sands.

Antioch Pow-wow.

Archie Blacksmith:
"Thank you for always
coming to the drum, to
honor the Movement
when that song was
sung, and for always
talking and sharing your
amusement and to
express your solidarity to
all of us urban folks!"
—John Whitefox.

Joyce Keoke and Buck Bone in the Community History Project archive.

"People in the urban areas know nothing about Indian people. And so if you go into a position where people begin to talk about their nationality, and you say that you are Indian, a lot of times the questions are so far out or curious that it makes people feel that— I mean, I've had people come up and ask me, 'What do you eat?' And I'm a Sioux from South Dakota, so I always tell them, 'Dog!'

"The Community History Project was an 'idea' that developed at IFH with Marilyn St. Germaine, Susan Lobo, and Gerri Martinez Lira. We wanted to record oral histories to leave to our future generations about what we experienced when we came on relocation to the Bay Area from small towns, rural areas, and reservations."
—*Gerri Martinez Lira*

I Am Indian

I am an Indian.
I am Tlinget.
I am a boy
Who likes baseball stickers.
I am a boy who likes baseball.
I am a boy who likes the Oakland A's.

—*Carlos Didrickson, Tlinget, Grade 2*

Skateboard

Once upon a time I was riding my skateboard down the hill.
My Dad called me to come and help him.
I turned and fell and broke my arm.

—Paul French, Nez Percé–Omaha, Grade 3

"Alcoholism and other drug addictions/diseases for the American Indian has been equal to any genocide wave of destruction of a race of a People on Mother Earth. We as American Indians must first look at ourselves as an individual to question where the alcoholism comes from and how it affects us today. Next is our own family, then our community. We have ancestral memory in each of us where there was a time that alcohol and other drugs were not in our lives. This is a strong resiliency factor.

"To heal from the disease of alcoholism takes all the work of our Indian pioneers who started the [treatment] center twenty-five years ago, the reawakening of our own Indian healing ceremonies, modern techniques, and today's effort to nurture and support Indian mothers with their children in a family healing from alcoholism."

—Betty N. Cooper, Executive Director, Family Healing Center

Betty always kept this poem hanging on the wall above her desk:

Akitchita

Paul Owns the Sabre

Go into the cities of stone, and
Look for them among the ruins;
You must stop what you are doing,
Then go, and take them back Home
To the land of Warriors.

"Being Indian is an honor and a responsibility. We must never forget our history and the contributions of our ancestors a century ago."

—*Martin Waukazoo, Executive Director, Native American Health Center*

How Ruby Saves Laughter

Esther G. Belin

for Les

I have a Ponca friend named Sailor
with a sweet windy voice that brushes away dirt and grime
you will know when you meet him
probably at the Hilltop on a Sunday after
you thought you'd never laugh
the sour stench from your stomach
out of your skull

Poncas got this magic
maybe it's the Oklahoma easy way of things
but Sailor sure sweeps me clean of dust
Whenever I see Sailor
I tell him
Take care of yo' skull, Sailor
'cause
Poncas
you see
are hard to find
so I say one more time
to my friend of three years
Sailor
you be careful
'cause
you see
Sailor is a Gentle Man
doin' time for the wrong reasons
so before I kiss his cheek *so long*

I give him a coffee can
tellin' him
Sailor
bein' an Indian's rough
bein' a Ponca's tougher
'cause
ain't hardly any around
so
when you get bruised and bloody again
you betta' collect your blood in this can
'cause
yo' blood's hard to come by
and more people need to laugh.

"Still Asleep after
Two Days."

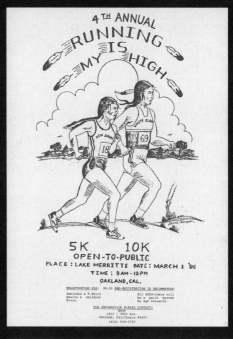

4 TH ANNUAL
RUNNING IS MY HIGH

5K   10K
OPEN-TO-PUBLIC
PLACE : LAKE MERRITTE   DATE : MARCH 1 '86
TIME : 9AM - 12PM
OAKLAND, CAL.

REGISTRATION FEE: $6.00   PRE-REGISTRATION IS RECOMMENDED

Includes a T.Shirt   ALL AGES/thers will
Adults & children   be a point system
Sizes.   by age category.

FOR INFORMATION PLEASE CONTACT:
NAAP
1815 - 39th Ave.
Oakland, California 94603
(415) 534-2737

12TH ANNUAL
"RUNNING IS MY HIGH"

5K & 10K Run, Walkers
March 12, 1994 Lake Merritt, Oakland, CA

Humor

Marilyn LaPlante St. Germaine

Humor is as essential in American Indian life as breathing is for life. Survival without humor must be very agonizing. Various kinds of humor can be found among Indian Peoples. Some humor is joyful, happy kidding; then some is harsh, teasing, joking, and shaming; or some is even just about everyday life. We laugh at self, family, clan, and tribal, racial, and cultural things.

Where I come from, Blackfeet Reservation in Montana, we are considered to have "sick" humor. An example of this is the housing for the elderly at home. When I moved home for a while from the Bay Area in 1984, my mother was living in a two-bedroom apartment in the elderly housing close by the hospital that was built in the late 1970s. I went to visit my cousin Carol Faye one day, and she asked, "Where are you staying?" I replied, "With my mom." My cousin got a big grin, began laughing, and said, "Oh, up on 'death row.' That's what we call the elderly apartments going up towards the hospital." We both really laughed. When I got home, I questioned my mother about where she lived. "Any particular name for the housing area here?" She said none that she knew of. I told her, "You guys live on death row! This is what Carol Faye had mentioned to me about the elderly housing." Mom responded, "Well, many of the people on the 'row' did die after moving here; the name fits good!"

Learning to laugh at one's self is one of the most healing remedies in the world. It's free; we all possess the power to do it, and it is so very enjoyable and can actually be catching. At any Indian community gathering, you can always hear bellows of laughter coming from each sacred direction. It is a most wonderful gift. Use it freely and frequently. It is very, very healing.

Even at sacred ceremonies, where the spiritual Interpreter sits before his altar, he at times tells us, the people, funny things the Spirits relay to him, and then he to us. The Spirits love happy, laughing humans. I have witnessed it, been a part of it, and know this happens daily in Indian communities. When there is something in life such as a death of a loved one, sometimes there seems to be no humor at all. Yet when one reflects back, the humor and laughter along with support, love, care, and acceptance eventually get one through. Humor brings you away from that very deep grief. It brings you out to remember that there is something more. My brother-in-law Sam passed away in August 1999. His brother Jess was telling Sam's eleven children, "That's the best damn wake and funeral I've ever been to. For four days, there was live music, dancing, food, and playing cards, many stories shared with family, friends, and foe. But, most of all, lots and lots of laughter. I hated this to end."

Another great source of humor among Indians is politics: Indian Politics. In the urban Indian world, it's with the governing boards for the nonprofit agencies. These are made up of various tribal memberships—all different, yet combined for strength and support, and sometimes lots and lots of friction.

I remember the time, not so long ago, 1995, one of the Indian agencies was having some community strife with the governing board. The community was coming forth to save the building because some of us had heard rumors that the director and board were thinking of selling the center. The Community History Project is housed there, and we, the Community History Project board, were concerned about some of the shady people who had attached themselves to the center. Then the community was denied access to the building; it was locked up, with the Community History Project archive materials inside. Because there was so much strife in the community, we all were very concerned that our history archive might be destroyed. Then the coordinator of the archives, Susan Lobo, a white woman and anthropologist, was allowed to return to her office. (This wonderful lady has helped create the only urban Indian history project in the United States. We have an invaluable resource, thanks to her unselfish efforts.) She began where she left off: gathering and archiving urban Indian history materials, while the community strife continued.

Then we heard that some of the people who had confronted the community were going through some boxes stored in the Community History Project office. There was a box labeled "Danny's" with some used clothing and some bones. Rumor spread that Susan Lobo, the anthropologist (!), had human bones in the Community History Project archive—Danny's bones. "I didn't know Danny died!" Some tribal beliefs about death involve taboos, especially about remains. Susan gracefully took the bones to be analyzed. They were deer bones made into awls for leather craft work. She even has a letter documenting this! She was not even aware that the bones had been there. A Plains tribe gentleman, Danny, needed to store a box with his things for a while when he went back home. Susan said, "Okay," but "for a while" ended up to be a few years. Anyway, Susan never did dig in the box, so when rumor spread that Danny's bones were in the Community History Project office, she was shocked and appalled. Once the dust settled, we laughed and laughed about this one and still retell it when we need another good laugh. It's become one of our Bay Area community stories, one of the crazy things that are a part of all of our lives here.

Christmas, about 1962.

American Indian

CHRISTMAS ART FAIRE

Indian Arts & Crafts   Door Prizes

Indian Food   Rummage sale

Cake Walk   Games

Gifts   Prizes

December 19th   10 a.m. · 4 p.m.
Pow-wow • Laney College • 7 p.m.

ART FAIRE at INTERTRIBAL FRIENDSHIP HOUSE
523 L. 14th St., Oakland, CA.   information: 452-1235

"Ever since I knew my mom, she was always on the board of directors at the Indian center, and she would always do things like the cooking, phoning, and she was always donating. Thanksgiving time came, and she would donate turkeys. Or Christmas time she'd make candies or get fruits."

    —Justine Buckskin

70   PART 3

My Father

My father
he taught me
how to fix
a car.
It was fun.
I checked
the oil
and the radiator. When
it was all
fixed we
went to
McDonalds
for lunch.

—Tara Skidders, Mohawk, Grade 5

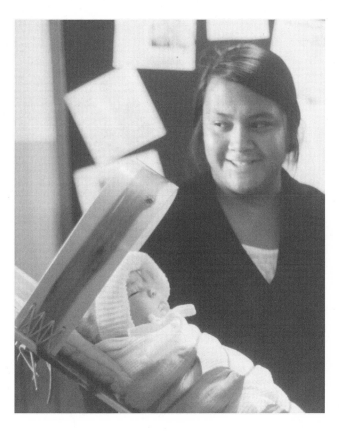

Adam with his baby,
Red House.

Our Families, Our
Children, about 1962.

My Grandmother

Clear shy breeze as my grandmother
Takes my hand for
A short walk which is her
Daily routine. It's not long
But short and cozy enough
Just to spend time with
My dearest grandmother.

—*Martha Weaselbear, Cheyenne/Arapahoe, Grade 12*

My Mom and Daddy

He's tall like a bear
And strong.
My mommy is soft like a pillow
And a blanket.
They are nice like a deer.
They make me feel happy
Like a baby bird.

—*Vickie Wilson*

"There are people who are important to me. They are the ones who I've gotten a lot of my guidance and knowledge from that I have now and that I can pass on to my own children. And just by knowing them, I can say they are a part of my family. That's where the friendship goes into family."

—*Lois Taylor*

"Even though we are going home, I don't really think we are completely just disappearing because I think of everything we've learned, and we're taking back a piece of somebody from the community, from the Elders down to the children. Everybody, it's like I said, is like my family."

—*Melinda Sanderson*

PART FOUR TIMES OF CHANGE

Throughout the 1960s, the Bay Area was a place of social change and ferment, and the Indian community became actively engaged in seeking social changes for the benefit of Indian people. The occupation of Alcatraz in 1969 was a landmark of consciousness for many, as was the Long Walk for Survival, the Spiritual Runs, and the many demonstrations and protests during this time. The social awareness of this period affected the structure, the leadership, and the power relationships within the Indian community.

In the late 1960s and early 1970s, a number of additional organizations were established, many of them educational, that recognized the expanding needs of the American Indian community in the Bay Area and drew on the creativity and energy of a generation that had grown up in the multitribal urban setting. For example, in the early 1970s a group of concerned parents in Oakland established a preschool that eventually evolved into Hintil Kuu Ca, which continues to provide academic and cultural classes for Indian children through the elementary grades.

IN COMMEMORATION OF THE 19th
ANNUAL WOUNDED KNEE MEMORIAL

February 27, 1992 is the 19th Anniversary of the Liberation of Wounded Knee, South Dakota by the American Indian Movement.

The American Indian Movement (AIM) International Indian Treaty Council (IITC) and the Leonard Peltier Defence Committee announce a Day of Commemoration beginning at 12:00 P.M. at the Federal Building 450 Golden Gate in San Francisco, There will be a number of speakers with the focus on Human Rights issues such as Forced Relocation of Native Peoples, Political Prisoners and other important issues.

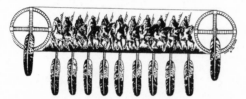

FEBRUARY 27TH, 1992
12:00 P.M. TO 1:00 P.M.

FEDERAL BUILDING
450 GOLDEN GATE
SAN FRANCISCO, CALIFORNIA

FOR MORE INFORMATION CONTACT (IITC) (415) 566-0251 OR (510) 825-6419

THE DENNIS BANKS BICENTENNIAL

CONTRIBUTIONS ARE NEEDED TO MEET DENNIS' $100,000 BAIL. PLEASE SEND ALL CONTRIBUTIONS TO;
THE DENNIS BANKS
LEGAL OFFENSE COALITION
P.O. BOX #601
OAKLAND, CA 94606
415-835-5644
A UNITED INDIAN PEOPLE MAKES A MIGHTY FIST!!!

Benefit Concert
for *AMERICAN INDIAN AIRLIFT*
Buffy St. Marie
Floyd Westerman & More

Thursday, Dec 3, 8:00 pm
Nourse Auditorium
Franklin & Hayes St., SF
Tickets: $8.00
(All BASS Outlets)

On Dec. 2, 1988 a massive airlift of food, medicines, warm clothing, tents, and building tools will begin to be sent to the Indian people now stranded in the Black Hills and at Big Mountain.
A truck will be outside Nourse Auditorium **before** the concert to collect food, medicine, blankets, clothing, etc.

Prepaid in association with the Bay Area International Collective.

Come to the monthly
BAY AREA REGIONAL MEETING
of Support Groups for the
NATIVE AMERICAN STRUGGLE

14 JULY
7:30

Updates and How to Get Involved:

A.I.M.	Leonard Peltier
Big Mountain	Go-Road
Yellow Thunder	D.Q. University
Native American Defense	Dennis Banks

American Indian Center 225 Valencia, S.F.

For more information or to have other issues added call 641-9010

"We would sit up about five or six hours every night, discussing things. We'd go over politics and history and Indian involvement here in the community and what we could do in the community. I was happy that I had learned to be around people and that I was becoming strong."
—*Melinda Sanderson*

Rosalie McKay-Want talks about her arrival on Alcatraz during the occupation:

"When we got to the pier, it was real dark by then, and there was a bonfire going, and Indians were standing around. Then we started walking up these stone steps, and it was a real long walk up. And the steps were high. And we were going along like that, and I heard some Indians talking in the background, and the sound of Indians is so different than when white people talk. And it felt so good; it just felt like I was home. And we ended up stayin' there just a long, long time." [Were women, as well as men, among the leaders of the occupation movement?] "Yes, they were. And there didn't seem to be any conflict. There was a good mix always. Women were involved in Alcatraz from the very beginning. Some of them swam from the boat going over for the first time. Women and men. Some of the Indian women had already been involved on community boards, like the San Francisco Indian Center board. A friend of mine, in particular. Her mother and a bunch of other women had started the Indian Center, and it was just like sitting around over coffee one day and saying, 'We ought to get together and get a place.' At Alcatraz, two people rose to the top as leaders: LaNada Means and Richard Oakes, one woman and one man."

THE NEWS MEDIA: ALCATRAZ OCCUPATION.

SF. CHRONICLE
14 Indians Invade, Claim Alcatraz
Nov 10, 1969
By Tim Findley

No. 315   HOME EDITION ••   TUESDAY, NOVEMBER 11, 1969

Indians 'Reserve' the Rock
Lehman Brightman

SF EXAMINER Nov. 21, 1969
Indians on Alcatraz Still Holding Out

—Unity Among Indians—   *Jan 12 1970*

Alcatraz Talks Make Little Headway

Invaders Say 'We'll Be Back'

Raiders Capture Alcatraz --A 'Free Indian Land'

Aftermath Of Alcatraz 'Invasion'

'Alcatraz Is Not an Island'
Ruth Teiser

ne government of the politics; second, let ians be the same as These proposals were eneral George Crook, ns be given the ballot. e the first battle at ch if Crook had lived n prevented. One can at if the work of the ho turned champion of h had been carried for- az had 80 years later the American Indian, Wounded Knee might

t an Island" presents eveloped by the Indi- r creating such a cen- rguments in favor of f sound so logical it dispute them in any icracese.

★ ★.

nple logic itself, like c of youth, is self- always reasons why done. Nevertheless, ies of this book will. desks of all members mmittee on National on, which is apparent- Alcatraz proposals in

this book than logic. of the Alcatraz occu-

pation and other more quickly abrogat- ed campaigns, together with paintings, photographs, poems and poetic prose ex- pressing the Indians' longing for unity, peace with all people, and peace with the earth. The volume's editor is Peter Blue Cloud, who was on Alcatraz during the 19 months the Indians lived there. He collect- ed the material and wrote some of it him- self, working closely with the publishers, Wingbow Press of Berkeley.

"Alcatraz is Not an Island" is the first book issued by this new firm, an out- growth of Book People, the distribution or- ganization that has been so strong a factor in the growth of California's smallbook publishers in recent years.

★ ★ ★

THE MATERIAL they distribute is ex- tremely diverse, ranging from "Practical Insight Meditation," by the Venerable Mahashi Sayadaw (Unity Press, $2.25), Skull Comix (Last Gasp Funnies, 50 cents), and Filipino Food by Ed Badajos (Olympia Press, $3.95) to liter- ary works like Robert Bly's "Point Reyes Poems" (Mudra, $1), Clifford Burke's "Griffin Creek" (Cranium Press, $3) and David Meltzer's "Knots" (Tree Books; $2).

"Alcatraz is Not an Island," with color reproductions in the text and on both pa- per covers, sells for $3.95; all royalties will go to the widow of Richard Oakes, the Indian militant who was slain last year in Sonoma county, and their seven children.

Getting Indians off Alcatraz Doesn't Solve the Problem
6-16-71

The remarkable patience of the Feder- al Government towards the Indian seizure of Alcatraz Island came finally to an end last Friday. The occupation of "the rock," begun in November, 1969, is no more.

In this final chapter of what could loosely be called the nation's "last Indian uprising," there was no alternative. For the government's public safety responsi- bilities must remain paramount.

Because the island's foghorns and 250,000 candlepower beacon had become inoperative, a hazard to navigation def- initely existed near the island.

Efforts to provide substitute warning devices simply proved inadequate, ac- cording to mariners' complaints, and no doubt the specter of a fully-loaded oil tanker piling up on the island shore was a constant nightmare to Coast Guard offi- cials.

Also, the hurling of rocks and poten- tially lethal missiles, and occasional fir- ing of weapons from the island were al- ways a threat to innocent sightseers or pleasure boaters sailing near the island.

Finally, the documented theft of gov- ernment property established that some of the occupants had strayed far from their originally announced purpose of es- tablishing an Indian cultural center on Al- catraz.

But if the orderly, non-violent re- taking of the historic island by federal of- ficials ended the immediate safety prob- lems, it only served to focus fresh atten- tion on the Federal Government's con- tinuing failure to find a solution to its 150-year-old "Indian problem."

Perhaps the government's reluctance to react precipitously to the occupation can be linked to the essentials of the Ind- ian enigma. As trustee of Indian lands, the United States is obliged to supply a home- site — a reservation — for American Indi- ans. Thus it perhaps didn't make much difference if this otherwise unused federal land was located in some remote wilder- ness or in the middle of San Francisco Bay. So why ask the Indians to leave?

Except that once public safety was threatened, or foibles committed, then action had to be taken to remove them from that particular "reservation."

The Alcatraz occupation, and the wan- ton destruction found after the Indians were removed, suggest the Federal Gov- ernment has in the main failed to provide a satisfactory environment for many tribes to live on their own lands and to retain their own cultures, and equally has not prepared many of them sufficiently to become part of this nation's social and economic life.

By word and by deed, the Indians' ac- tions, while not excusable, must be inter- preted as a rather pathetic protest against a government policy that is at once paternalistic and indifferent.

However it is developed as part of the proposed Golden Gate National Recrea- tion Area, Alcatraz Island will long re- main a source of inspiration and hope to all those native Americans who believe their cause is just and that they are enti- tled to better treatment at the hands of the "great white father."

Supplies Arrive
Indians Reinforced --U.S. Delays Action

Indians' Bleak Winter

Page 18 Section A ☆☆☆☆ S. F. Sunday Examiner & Chronicle, November 23, 1969

Foggy Sea Blockade Strands Alcatraz Indians

14 Indians Invade, Claim Alcatraz

By Tim Findley

Alcatraz was occupied late yesterday by 14 young American Indians who "reclaimed" the island and vowed to stay on it until authorities recognize Indian rights to the bleak piece of property.

The twilight invasion followed a colorful assault on the island yesterday afternoon by 50 Indians who borrowed a Canadian clipper ship to circle The Rock twice.

Four young braves dived off the barque Monte Cristo and swam to shore during that assault, but were taken back off again by a friendly yachtsman after a caretaker threatened to summon United States marshals.

The Chronicle learned last

Craig, 37, of Vancouver, the owner-captain of the 138-foot barque Monte Cristo.

Craig, who said he agreed to lend his $500,000 ship "because we sympathize with the underdog," even fired a few blank rounds from the vessel's cannons to lend authenticity as the war-whooping Indians circled the island.

Craig kept his passengers about 100 yards offshore, however. Although four or five stalwarts who jumped from the ship made it to shore and briefly claimed the island, it appeared that the Indians would have to settle for less than complete victory.

Indian spokesmen declined,

See Back Page

—From Page 1

the day huddled around fires, cooking turkey for a feast — "don't call it Thanksgiving" one Indian cautioned — or watching the boats maneuver in the fog.

All seemed in good spirits, including at least four children who played hide-and-seek in the tiny cell blocks where the federal government had once disciplined its most unruly prisoners.

One youngster — Denyon Means, 2, known to the Indians as the Alcatraz Kid — needed a baby bottle, according to his mother LaNada Means of San Francisco. Otherwise the children seemed to be enjoying the holiday.

Three of the Indians — students like many of the other demonstrators — wanted to

leave Alcatraz but the Coast Guard refused to allow them to board the launch or allow civilian vessels close enough to pick up passengers.

Friday night a motorized sloop from Sausalito brought food to the island but yesterday it was turned away.

From a pole at dockside flew the Red Power flag depicting a broken peace pipe and a teepee.

Watch TV

Water and electricity were still functioning and a group of the demonstrators spent the early afternoon watching the Michigan-Ohio State football game on television.

Others played softball or whiled away the time tossing a Frisbee.

"The government is going to have to realize we mean business," said Richard

Oakes, who has acted as leader of the invaders. "We are not just children or wards of the state.

"What we are seeking as Indians is a real meaning in life, a challenge."

'Respect Ourselves'

Oakes, a husky young man with thick black hair, paused for a moment and looked out at the foggy bay.

"This is a technological age," he said. "but Indians are more down to earth. We have a greater respect for what we have ourselves and this is what we are trying to build here.

"We will talk to (Interior Secretary Walter) Hickel, but only if he comes out here. We won't talk to him on the telephone if he calls and we won't talk with a middle-man.

Alcatraz Participant Richard Oakes Shot to Death at California YMCA CAMP

NAVAJO TIMES   October 12, 1972

Invaders Claim Rock Is Theirs

PROCLAMATION:

To the Great White Father and All His People —

We, the native Americans, re-claim the land known as Alcatraz Island in the name of all American Indians by right of discovery.

We, wish to be fair and honorable in our dealings with the Caucasian inhabitants of this land, and hereby offer the following treaty:

We will purchase said Alcatraz Island for twenty-four dollars (24) in glass beads and red cloth, a precedent set by the white man's purchase of a similar island about 300 years ago. We know that $24 in trade goods for these 16 acres is more than was paid when Manhattan Island was sold, but we know that land values have risen over the years. Our offer of $1.24 per acre is greater than the 47 cents per acre the white men are now paying the California Indians for their land.

We will give to the inhabitants of this island a portion of the land for their own to be held in trust by the American Indian Affairs and by the bureau of Caucasian Affairs to hold in perpetuity — for as long as the sun shall rise and the rivers go down to the sea. We will further guide the inhabitants in the proper way of living. We will offer them our religion, our education, our life-ways, in order to help them achieve our level of civilization and thus raise them and all their white brothers up from their savage and unhappy state. We offer this treaty in good faith and wish to be fair and honorable in our dealings with all white men.

We feel that this so-called Alcatraz Island is more than suitable for an Indian reservation, as determined by the white man's own standards. By this we mean that this place resembles most Indian reservations in that:

1. It is isolated from modern facilities, and without adequate means of transportation.
2. It has no fresh running water.
3. It has inadequate sanitation facilities.
4. There are no oil or mineral rights.
5. There is no industry and so unemployment is very great.
6. There are no health care facilities.
7. The soil is rocky and non-productive, and the land does not support game.
8. There are no educational facilities.

9. The population has always exceeded the land base.
10. The population has always been held as prisoners and kept dependent upon others.

Further, it would be fitting and symbolic that ships from all over the world, entering the Golden Gate, would first see Indian land, and thus be reminded of the true history of this nation. This tiny island would be a symbol of the great lands once ruled by free and noble Indians.

What use will we make of this land?

Since the San Francisco Indian Center burned down, there is no place for Indians to assemble and carry on tribal life here in the white man's city. Therefore, we plan to develop on this island several Indian institutions:

1. A Center for Native American Studies which will educate them to the skills and knowledge relevant to improve the lives and spirits of all Indian peoples.
2. An American Indian Spiritual Center which will practice our ancient tribal religious and sacred healing ceremonies . . .
3. An Indian Center of Ecology which will train and support our young people in scientific research and practice to restore our lands and waters to their pure and natural state. . .
4. A Great Indian Training School will be developed to teach our people how to make a living in the world, improve our standard of living, and to end hunger and unemployment among all our people . . .

Some of the present buildings will be taken over to develop an AMERICAN INDIAN MUSEUM which will depict our native food & other cultural contributions will have given to the world. Another part of the museum will present some of the things the white man has given to the Indians in return for the land and life he took: disease, alcohol, poverty and cultural decimation (As symbolized by old tin cans, barbed wire, rubber tires, plastic containers, etc.) . . .

In the name of all Indians, therefore, we re-claim this island for our Indian nations. . .

Signed,
Indians of All Tribes
November 1969
San Francisco, California

The 1989 American Indian Film Festival is dedicated to the *Spirit of Alcatraz* — to the Indian participants and non-Indian supporters who stood together — learned and shared — twenty years ago.

"This will be the tenth anniversary [1979], and we are thinking of a bunch of us getting together and doing an Alcatraz reunion. We are thinking of all the people that went through, and I said, 'I wish we had the list of everybody who was there.'"

—*Justine Buckskin*

AMERICAN INDIANS ON ALCATRAZ ISLAND

FEB 11, 1979

CEREMONIES ON THE INTERNATIONAL DAY OF SOLIDARITY FOR ALL NATIVE POLITICAL PRISONERS, AND TO COMMEMORATE THE LONGEST WALK.

THE BOAT WILL LEAVE FOR ALCATRAZ AT 7:00 AM. AND WILL RETURN AT 10:30 AM. TICKETS: ADULTS $2.00, CHILDREN $1.00, 350 PEOPLE MAX. AT 11:00 AM THERE WILL BE A WALK FROM PIER #43 TO MARKS MEADOW IN GOLDEN GATE PARK. WHERE A RALLY WILL TAKE PLACE FROM 1:00 PM TO 5:00 PM. 24TH AVE. & FULTON, THERE WILL AMERICAN INDIAN SPEAKERS. MUSIC WILL BE PROVIDED BY NATIVE AMERICAN GROUPS. LET ALL FOUR SACRED COLORS; RED, YELLOW, BLACK AND WHITE COME TOGETHER ONCE AGAIN TO PRAY AND GIVE SUPPORT TO ALL NATIVE POLITICAL PRISONERS ON THIS OUR MOTHER EARTH. THE BENEFIT WILL BE HELD FROM 7:30PM TO MIDNIGHT AT EVERETTE JR HIGH SCHOOL 450 CHURCH AVE SAN FRANCISCO. FOR MORE INFORMATION CALL ANY OF THESE NUMBERS; 261-2899, 533-4300 OR 658-7128

ALCATRAZ
10 YEARS AFTER

PRESENTING...

A REUNION

HAPPENING......

NOVEMBER 18, 1979   10am UNTIL 6pm

STERNGROVE PARK, SAN FRANCISCO, CALIFORNIA

POT LUCK! BRING ENOUGH FOR YOUR FAMILY AND

ENOUGH TO SHARE WITH FRIENDS....

(for further information contact Lola Pepion 536-8446

Suzanne Regimbal 552-4917

(AREA CODE 415)

Sunrise at Alcatraz

to commemorate
"The International Year of the World's Indigenous Peoples"

Monday, October 11, 1993
5:30 AM to 9 AM

Remember Indigenous
past origins of Alcatraz
Security - w/call tx 1/R

> words of wisdom
> songs of strength
> drumming
> memories of past generations
> reaffirmations
> working for the unborn
& solidarity messages

special cultural presentation

Boats leave Pier 41
• 5:30 AM
• 6:00 AM
• 6:15 AM

contact:
RED & WHITE FLEET (415) 546-2700
at PIER 41, Fisherman's Wharf, SF
TICKETS: $8 (age 12 and under FREE)

Sponsored by
International Indian Treaty Council
123 Townsend St., Suite 575
San Francisco, CA 94107-1907   PH: (415) 512-1501 FAX: (415) 512-1507

(No drugs or weapons, please)

The Long Walk for
Survival, starting from
Alcatraz Island, 1980.
A walk against hunger,
the draft, nuclear energy,
and weapons.

Alcatraz veterans and
longtime community
members at the thirtieth
anniversary celebration
of the occupation of
Alcatraz. *Front:* Joe
Morris. *Back, left to right:*
Eileen Bastian, Doug
Duncan, Shirley Garcia,
John Whitefox.

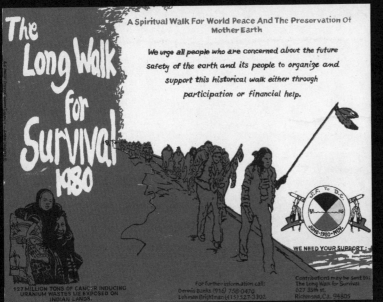

A Spiritual Walk For World Peace And The Preservation Of Mother Earth

We urge all people who are concerned about the future safety of the earth and its people to organize and support this historical walk either through participation or financial help.

WE NEED YOUR SUPPORT:

127 MILLION TONS OF CANCER INDUCING URANIUM WASTES LIE EXPOSED ON INDIAN LANDS.

For further information call:
Dennis Banks (916) 758-0470
Lehman Brightman (415) 527-3302

Contributions may be sent to:
The Long Walk for Survival
627 35th st.
Richmond, Ca. 94805

The people in this American nation state must act. The rights of the people are more important than the rights of the government. The future of the coming generations is at stake. We pray for the people.

FREE PELTIER

THE WOMEN'S INDIGENOUS NETWORK

Medicine men Phillip Deer (right), and Hopi elder Thomas Banyaca (far left) at Intertribal Friendship House gathering

Staff photo by Lonnie Wilson

American Indians' spiritual rebirth

"When we came over here to the Bay Area, I had never been up this far north. So it was all new. And they were going to put us in the training program for a trade. What I did was sign a paper, and I'm still curious about what I signed away. We went through a lot of adjustments here. It didn't take very long for some people to more or less give up hope, I guess. And they would leave. In three months' time, only half of us were here. It depended on what trade you went into. I went into drafting."

—*Byron Sanderson*

"I've always got a job. They always need welders, a certain kind of welder. I like to travel to a certain extent, like looking for work or working in different locations. You stay a while in one place and go to another place and get acquainted with another environment. But I don't like to travel from state to state. I did go to Los Angeles a few times—go down there and check around on the Indians."
—*Leonard Smith*

"I'm a very fortunate man to have taken part in the Oakland community with my life. And I want to inspire the younger people and the guys down in the park, the ones in jail, the ones in prison. Hey, you know, 'Old Wahpepah was the same thing, and now look, he's got a gourd in his hand.' The gourd. If there was something to inspire people with my life, I would like to inspire young people to take part in taking care of their people."
—*Bill Wahpepah*

Press conference after the AIM Survival School fire, 1979. *Left to right:* ——, Tawna Sanchez, ——, Bill Wahpepah, ——, Betty Cooper.

"My dad had a good life. My dad tried to stop the war, but he just died. He had a good, fun time. Let me tell you a part about him. He was a funny person. Every day he went swimming. My dad came to my school and talked about Indians. My dad loved being Indian. He worked hard."
    —*Rencho Wahpepah (Kickapoo/Sac Fox/Ojibwa)*

Dedication Poem for Oche Watt Te Ou/Reflection
Performed at Yerba Buena Gardens, San Francisco, October 17, 1993

Dennis Jennings

Now that
most of the Ohlones
are under our feet
too few left to recognize,
whole families going unrecognized,
as city officials discuss with a Russian
what to do with the old military land.
OHLONES
(as if they ever called themselves that until lately)
lived here (at this place) in the Garden of Eden,
still live among us (these genetic remnants),
these all too human original people of this place.

All different races of tribes live here now—
only one or two generations removed from their lands.
INDIANS
all around you now,
Some, right beside you in the spirit world.
Some, right beside you on the bus.
Some tending your gardens,
some growing your food,
some cleaning your houses,
some—with really good jobs working at middle management.
All crying for expression—wanting you to see them,
hear them—
listen!

Listen to all we cannot say to you while you cannot see
yourselves in the mirror,
this topsy-turvy world nowadays—putting animals in zoos to
save them.
The animal nations, too, long gone on to other places,
just a few like raccoons & opossums & hawks
holding ground and sky
against this metropolitan interlope—
this industry-commerce clique
buying their way on,
flags progress.

Relocated winos once lived here too.
No more South Park.
No more Taber or Varney Addresses.
Just where's the neighborhood?
Now that these edifices are here—
for our own edification—
the long hope that other cultures can teach us,
that Art can heal us,
(all these wounds we continue to inflict on our own species,)
that Art can soothe us and balm us,
can help us reclaim the human among and within us,
that these cultures from around the world can teach us and
save us,
now that commerce&industry&information
has subdued and extinguished all these ancient fires,
now that we are all prisoner, we will be free
through Art, Culture!

Ishi
saw it here—
maybe at this very spot—
hustling, bustling
big city ambition, an old city-state plot,
Megopolis even now taking mega bites of our Mother Earth,
selling space even now in space,
turning profit margins on futures,
whose futures?
Maybe Art can save us, the humans,
maybe we can save ourselves

listening to other cultures
(or what's left of them after the oil pipeline,
the diamond mine, the coal seams,
the radioactive tailings
run them down, run them off).
Hard to say if Art can save us
in a place where helicopters become flying angels and both are
mirages—
laser fantasies.
Hard to say if we can learn in time.
Hard to say if the artists can teach us,
if this voice, or that look,
or this music, or that image,
or these hands
will teach us to respect life,
to begin to own our own lives,
to cherish life all life all ways,
that all babies eat everyday.
Hard to say if we arrived on time to save ourselves.
Nowadays kids killings kids everywhere,
wars grind on.
Nowadays drugs claiming lives on all sides,
wars grind on.
Nowadays other plagues spreading,
C (see), I (eye), AIDS stalking victims,
the war grinds on.
Maybe some baby born today has an answer.
Hope she's on time.
Maybe today some child is born somewhere way off
and against all odds he lives
to teach us all.
Hope they can afford to live around here by that time.
Maybe all these people of all these races and cultures will
teach seeking peace
with the Earth
and with ourselves.
Maybe some day way off
from Somalia & Haiti, from Bolivia to South Africa, from
Cambodia to West Papua,
from Bougainvillia to Appalachia, from Pine Ridge to

Crescent Valley, Nevada,
We'll all have a profit sharing plan,
that we will all share Mother Earth,
that we will all share Mother Earth and her bounty equally,
that all babies eat,
and grow to learn,
and grow to teach;
We shall see.

We may yet see . . .

THE INTERNATIONAL INDIAN TREATY COUNCIL
PRESENTS

"REEL INDIANS"

AN EVENING OF FILMS

Launching the Observance of 500 Years of Indian Resistance to Colonization
1492-1992
and the Centennial Commemoration of the Massacre
at Wounded Knee, South Dakota
Dec. 29,1890

SATURDAY NOVEMBER 24
American Indian Center
225 Valencia St. S.F.

"BRAVE HEARTED WOMAN: the story of Anna Mae Aquash"
Anna Mae was an A.I.M. activist who was mysteriously murdered in 1976.
"TO PROTECT MOTHER EARTH" - Broken Treaty II
- narrated by Robert Redford.
Tells of the Western Shoshone and their efforts to re-claim their Ancestral Lands
now being used as a Nuclear Test Site.

7:00 P.M.   Donation $7.00
Red Sky Singers -AIM Drum
M.C. BILL MEANS

REMEMBER WOUNDED KNEE!
For Information: 566-0251

In Memory of those Who
Have Come Before Us

1890-1990
100 Year Anniversary of the
Wounded Knee Massacre
by the U.S. 7th Cavalry

Carrying on That Way

Janeen Antoine

Lately I've heard various Native friends express their feelings that the San Francisco Bay Area is a special place and holds their heart because there is so much going on culturally. I first arrived here bound for college in 1973, with no idea what California was about, but ready to give it a try. Coming from the South Dakota boonies, I suppose I left partly for the adventure. There was some allure to the notion of traveling and seeing different places, and California had a certain mystique at the time with all the hippie vans invading Indian country.

Here I learned of the diversity of the California Native and relocated community, through exposure, travel, and time. I soon learned there were many tribes in California and soon also learned of the many relocated and indigenous tribal people who lived here. Most often the contact was through pow-wows, a familiar celebration from home, but one that had new elements out here. It is a blending of all types of art forms—food, music, songs, regalia, dance, ceremony, and socializing—where tipi creeping and 49-ing evolved into high art forms! There were so many different tribes—from Arizona, Oklahoma, California, Nevada, all participating in these social gatherings.

Eventually I became exposed to many other art forms, and it was the contact with the individuals doing this art that had a great impact on me and made me so happy to be involved with the Native cultural community. From sweats, pow-wows, and sun dances, to Big Times, Strawberry Festivals, and roundhouse ceremonies, there is always something happening. In the past several decades, there has been a mushrooming of cultural events. Exhibits, music concerts, book readings, film screenings, dances, demonstrations, performances—there's something going on every week. The arts, whatever that means, are active and well. Like ocean waves breaking one after the next, like the inevitability of every new morning sun, many individuals and groups rise to work within our community and will always carry on that way.

There are many folks to recognize for their cultural activism in the Bay Area. All of the dancers, drummers, singers, artists, and behind-the-scenes organizers who participate in our pow-wows must certainly be acknowledged for their love of Native music, dances, and songs. The Costos created the American Indian Historical Society in San Francisco, published the American Indian Storyteller reader series, and helped some of the early artists such as Leatrice Mikkelson and George Longfish. George was especially active as an artist and activist, instrumental in promoting Native artists through the C. N. Gorman Museum in Davis and in helping to get American Indian Contemporary Arts (AICA) established.

Over the years, the South of Market Cultural Center has been home to a number of Native groups, including Jean McLean's American Indian Workshop, AICA, Debora Iyall's Inkclan, and more recently the Native American Cultural Center. Mike Smith's American Indian Film Festival has been a true focal point of the Native community and provides an opportunity to share the pride in our Native talent, as has the Stanford Pow-wow, both now in existence for more than twenty-five years. Other historic markers are the radio programs *Living on Indian Time* (on KPFA) and *Webworks: Voices of the Indian Nation* (on KPOO), which Mary Jane and Tavia have worked with for so many decades. Malcolm Margolin's wonderful *News from Native California* brings us much cultural information about the resilient California Indian Peoples, about their arts and lifeways, and about the abundant work they are doing on language restoration, basketry, cultural activism, and all areas of Native life today. The International Indian Treaty Council's yearly Alcatraz gathering and the Indigenous People's Day Parade in Berkeley—organized by our dear friend Millie Ketcheshawno these past ten years—have also both become signature cultural events that are now associated with the Bay Area activist history. Any reckoning of this sort would not be complete without the Intertribal Friendship House (IFH), one of the oldest Native community centers in the country. The IFH has weathered many storms and still serves as a haven for community gatherings, dances, films, socials, celebrations, and mournings. In all our comings and goings, everyone at some time has gone to IFH for an event of some sort.

More recently formed organizations in San Francisco within the past ten years include the California Indian Museum and the Native American Cultural Center of San Francisco, both searching to find a home of some sort in San Francisco. In the greater Bay Area, the California Indian Storytellers Association, the California Indian Basketweavers Association, and Gathering Tribes are also newer arrivals that have contributed much to the cultural landscape of the Bay Area.

When Ken Banks and I started AICA in 1983, we wanted to show the Bay Area the diversity and creativity of the Native community and some of the positive contributions Native Peoples have made. It has been organizing and promoting exhibits and events since then—showing the public the works of artists from across the country and helping to dispel the misinformation and stereotypes that all Indians live in tipis, chase buffaloes, weave Navajo rugs, make pueblo jewelry, and paint southwestern landscapes. Artists have been encouraged to explore their own cultural identities and to escape from the bondage of what collectors and the public at large envision as Native American art and more importantly as Native American Peoples. The diversity is abundant, and it has been a great pleasure exploring and promoting this diversity as AICA's director since 1987.

The AICA gallery has shown the works of or promoted many artists who have had some connection to the Bay Area, such as San Francisco Art Institute alums Fritz Scholder, T. C. Cannon, Linda Lomahaftewa, Steven Deo, Mario Martinez, and Zig Jackson. Other feathered artists with Bay Area history have included John Balloue, Hulleah Tsinhnahjinnie, Paul Owns the Sabre, R. C. Gorman, Frank LaPena, Chuna McIntyre, Jean LaMarr, L. Frank Manriquez, Ed NoiseCat, Sara Bates, Parris Butler, Kevin Red Star, Julian Lang, Brian Tripp, Celeste Conners, and Rabbett Strickland. So many additional talented, wonderful artists from across the country have truly enriched and blessed us with their work that it is impossible to name them all. We are simply fortunate to have had the gallery here to enjoy all their work. Where AICA goes from here is the question of the day because we have been "dot-commed" (my new expletive) out of our former location.

Longtime artists and activists John Trudell and Floyd Westerman have both, happily for us, been regular fixtures here in the Bay Area as well. Performing artists such as Lanny Pinola, Gina Pacaldo, Gilbert Blacksmith, Doug Duncan, WithOut Rezervation, Walter Johnson, and Eddie Madril have also represented us well within the greater community. Poets such as Duane Big Eagle, Ramona Wilson, Muriel Antoine, Michael Marin, and Heath St. John have graced us with their words. Other artists, such as filmmakers Jim Fortier and Peter Bratt and musician John Carlos Perea, are making our voices heard in new ways to new audiences.

All these current artists and all the artists to come will continue to work, and the vehicles to support them will evolve and form as needed and able in order to express this essential cultural affirmation and our existence as Native Peoples. But probably the biggest cultural contribution comes from each one of us who in some way upholds our traditions, maintains our ties, and continues in a positive and sharing manner to explore and affirm who we are. We have to thank our Creator for our existence, our ancestors for our survival, and the Ohlone Peoples for the lands we occupy and for the opportunity to do so in this beautiful place.

—22nd ANNUAL—
AMERICAN INDIAN FILM FESTIVAL®

OPENING WEEKEND
NOVEMBER 6 - 8, 1997
PALACE OF FINE ARTS
3301 Lyon Street, San Francisco

➤ **NOVEMBER 6 & 7**
7:30 PM   TIX: $7.00

➤ **NOVEMBER 8**
7:30 PM   TIX: $10.00
• AMERICAN INDIAN MOTION PICTURE
AWARDS CEREMONY

• *KASHTIN* [Innu Nation Quebec]
Internationally reknown recording
artists will perform in concert
SCREENING, AWARDS, & CONCERT

➤ **NOVEMBER 10 & 11**
❖ Native American
Film Finance Forum
Goethe Institut - San Francisco

INDIANS MAKE MOVIES© Michael Horse 1996

Claude McKenzie   Florent Vollant

✳ American Indian Film Festival continues thru November 20th at other venues ✳

Produced by the American Indian Film Institute (AIFI), a non-profit media-arts and education organization, the American Indian Film Festival® is the *oldest* and *most prestigious* festival of it's kind in the world. Founded in 1975, the festival has screened more than 500 films in the past two decades, from a wide variety of filmmakers, premiering major studio releases as well as the work of the more adventurous independents.

The American Indian Film Festival is unique in that it is truly a Native American media presentation, founded and produced by American Indian people. As such, the festival takes particular pride in presenting documentaries and dramas that come from within the Native community itself, and in supporting the work of new and emerging Native American actors, writers and filmmakers. In many cases, the festival is an important stepping stone for them to other national and international venues.

The American Indian Film Festival is the focal point of our year-round exhibition program, and leads our strategy to improve the distribution of films *by* and *about* American Indians, to develop a marketplace in which Indian media artists can cultivate financial resources for production and distribution, and to open up a network for technical support and resource-sharing among Indian producers, directors, writers, actors/performers and craftspeople. Combining education with celebration, the American Indian Film Festival brings the rich cultural heritage and diversity of our nation's *first people* into a forum where it can be shared with the larger community via the magic of the silver screen, and all the power of good storytelling.

INFO: 415. 554-0525   E-MAIL: AIFISF@AOL.COM

**10th Annual
American Indian
Film Festival**

COYOTE

The Director ©1985 Harry Fonseca

November 14-16, 1985
Palace of Fine Arts   San Francisco, CA

**6th ANNUAL
AMERICAN INDIAN FILM FESTIVAL**
November 5-7, 1981
Palace of Fine Arts, San Francisco
Tickets $4.00 General/$3.00 Students & Senior Citizens
Tickets at BASS and at the door. Information: 552-1070

Tawna Sanchez and
Cathy Kanapa at the
1980 American Indian
Music Festival at the San
Francisco Indian Center.

AMERICAN INDIAN MUSIC FESTIVAL 1982

PALACE of FINE ARTS
San Francisco, California

FEBRUARY 19, 20, 21

Master of Ceremonies **Max Gail**

Star of T.V. Series "BARNEY MILLER"

Musicians **FLOYD WESTERMAN**
PAUL ORTEGA & SHARON BURCH
and many local musicians
Contemporary American Indian Art Show

Arts & Crafts

For more information, call (415) 452 1235

Admission
Adult $7
Senior/child $5
Fri. Sat. 7 p.m.
Sun. 3 p.m.

American Indian Music Festival

Saturday JUNE 27 1992

GATES OPEN: 10 AM
FESTIVAL ENDS: 6 PM
ESTUARY PARK, OAKLAND
EMBARCADERO & FALLON STREETS
ADJACENT TO JACK LONDON SQUARE

TRADITIONAL & CONTEMPORARY INDIAN MUSIC · NATIVE CRAFTS SHOW & SALE

TICKETS: $6.00 DAY OF SHOW; $5.00 ADVANCE TICKETS AVAILABLE AT INTERTRIBAL FRIENDSHIP HOUSE
PRODUCED BY AND BENEFITTING INTERTRIBAL FRIENDSHIP HOUSE, 523 E. 14TH STREET, OAKLAND, CA 94606. FOR INFO: (510) 452-1235.
SUPPORTED BY A GRANT FROM THE OAKLAND ARTS COUNCIL.

PART FIVE CREATING A COMMUNITY FOR FUTURE GENERATIONS

Throughout the 1980s and 1990s, increased diversity within the Bay Area Indian community has continued and is reflected in the range of organizations and activities that exist. The original migrants in the city during the 1930s to 1950s have become the grandparent generation; some by now have even become great-grandparents. In contrast to events and tactics of the late 1960s and the 1970s, those who address political and social issues are less likely to focus on demonstrations or takeovers and more likely to use the courts, education, and influence to sway thinking. These approaches exemplify elements in an overall strategy for cultural survival in the city.

Throughout its history, the most outstanding dynamics of the community have been the way in which it has created and sustained organizations that answer fundamental social needs; the ways that identity has been both maintained and transformed in this urban multi-tribal setting; the ways that fundamental values and spirituality have found expression in an urban context; and the consistent features of tribal cultures that have come to be the basis for the community. The ability of Indian people to maintain these dynamics has helped us to persist and flourish. This is the ability to create, re-create, and transform a community for future generations.

Growing Up Indian

Ramona Wilson

Although a thousand miles and decades separate me and my schooling experience from that of young people today, we are alike. For we are Indian, these young people and I. For they, as I once did, struggle to make sense of their lives and struggle to see, in schools and books, an image of who they are.

I grew up in the country, on the Colville Indian reservation in Washington State. To go to school, I walked through fields to catch the yellow bus that crossed the river into town. The public school there, in its teachings and its population, was a foreign country. There were only a few of us Indians, for most of the families sent their children to the mission boarding school up in Omak. The history I was taught left me in silent bewilderment and with an anger I couldn't verbalize or focus. I could not feel pride for the brave settlers who fought weather and Indians to fulfill their dreams of land and prosperity. When the settlers won a battle, it was a victory, but when Indians won, it was a massacre. When studying local history, our classes took field trips to the "first" river landing, the "first" buildings. Never did I learn about the history of the people who had already lived there for centuries, who had established travel and trade routes into Canada and Oregon and to the Pacific and into the Plains. I was invisible and voiceless in my ignorance of my own people.

I was a good student, but school had no hold on me. Instead, in the fall when I was seventeen, there were dollars to be earned in the apple orchards, new jeans and shoes to be bought, and good times to be found. But, fortunately, our tribe had an education officer, and one September day he came out to the orchard to get me to apply to the Institute of American Indian Arts in Santa Fe, New Mexico. It took several trips on his part, but at last all parts of the application were complete. One month later I came to the place that would really educate me. *To educate* means, after all, to lead, and I began to be led onto the road of knowing about my people and myself. For the first time, I felt the immensity and power of the

Indian world, its range, its language and music, its history. Here was my place, and for the first time I viewed my land and people through eyes that respected and valued them, and that respected and valued me. For the first time, I had Indian teachers.

My early educational experience is not much different than what I see now for many American Indian students in Oakland and the surrounding communities. The schools many attend are predominately of one culture or another, such as black, Latino, or Asian, but never American Indian. Current multicultural education curricula are generally built around the unit method of teaching, where, for example, a Native American unit is taught for a few weeks in November and a Mexican American unit might be taught in May. The language of the unit uses terms such as *they* or *the Indians*. Always, I think, for the Indian child, there is the sense that someone far away is attempting to speak about deeply personal and crucially important matters. That someone speaks of those important things as one would speak about life forms in the ocean or about the strange customs of extinct civilizations. So, for that Indian child, a unit about the Indians will be as meaningful as one about ancient Greece or Rome. Indian youth of today, as young people always must, struggle to form an identity. Part of that identity formation is the question of being Indian. Current school curricula often only further confuse or alienate the student with third-person language and inaccurate or simplistic treatments of cultural subjects.

Before they can appreciate and move freely and confidently in a multicultural curriculum, they must know their own histories, their own lives, and find their own voices. I believe this is best done through the ways that appeal to young people and, in fact, are the ways that young people in tribal life learn their traditions. Art, music, stories, and observation of their Elders are ways that seek the heart as well as the mind. As young people view the art or listen to songs and stories, they, too, have a great desire to create, and, in creating, they maintain and pass on our Indian ways. "Indian ways" refers to a way of thinking, a way of being in the world.

Some scenes come to mind. In one, children from many tribes come together at Hintil Kuu Ca, the American Indian Child Development Center in Oakland. They listen to and read poems by well-known Indian poets. They learn about the writer, see the books he or she has published. Then they write their own poems, inspired by the beauty of the words and what they have learned. For many, this is their first positive and moving experience with writing and literature.

In another scene, children view pictures and videos about traditional forms of American Indian art and see how contemporary artists have drawn on their tribal heritage to create pieces of art that set standards for the entire art world to follow. Then they, too, with excitement and great concentration begin their own artwork. Later, when these pieces are exhibited, in Oakland's Museum of Children's Art or at the city's annual Art Festival at the Lake, adults are surprised to see how young these artists are who show such talent and power of thought.

And in still another scene, twenty-four youth gather once a month at Intertribal Friendship House for the Math, Engineering, and Science Achievement (MESA) Program. Founded at Oakland Technical High School, MESA seeks to raise the number of underrepresented minorities in the fields of math and science. Under the direction of the Indian Education Center, students participate in fun, hands-on group activities that teach basic science and math concepts, and they learn to work in groups and to support each other as learners. They also become acquainted with careers in these fields. For American Indian youth, the students gain a perspective they will not get in the schools. They learn about the contributions of their tribal peoples and about Indian mathematicians and scientists, but, most of all, they are encouraged to think of themselves as learners, as potential scholars. For them, the message is overt: that they, too, can succeed at universities but still be proudly Indian.

Epilogue

The preceding part of this essay was first composed around 1993. As I read back over it, I am struck by the optimism and belief that great things were happening in the education of American Indians in Oakland. Does this spirit still exist? What changes have occurred?

Now, at the turn of a new millennium, I can say that the spirit does yet exist, but I am surprised that many things have not changed. For example, an American Indian curriculum in Oakland public schools remains as weak or nonexistent as it ever was, but several literature textbooks now feature excerpts from nationally known writers such as M. Scott Momaday or Leslie Silko, and text-book-adoption committees are careful to include American Indian people. However, the number of American Indian teachers and administrators in the school system remains small.

The resources that have come into the community have increased. The California Indian Education Center (IEC) that provides supplemental services has continued to grow in its annual budget and now can offer specialist-level academic support, computer education, a library, and other amenities that were only a dream six years ago. The MESA program that the IEC offers now has a real budget that supports its own coordinator and a complete precollege advising, academic support, and enrichment program.

The Oakland Unified School District Office of Indian Education has survived, retaining its office and library through times when there were attempts to cut it from the district budget. Its staff, although smaller, has continued its advocacy and assistance to Indian youth and their families. Hintil Kuu Ca also continues to provide early-childhood and after-school care for many Indian families.

One of the most important changes since 1993 has been the addition of the American Indian Public Charter School in Oakland. The charter school movement in California was legislated into being in 1992. The intent of the legislation was to create a tool for school reform and to serve populations that were not meeting with success. The more promising possibilities for the American Indian community were the inclusion of teachers and parents and students in the decision-making processes of the charter school and the freedom for the school to design curriculum and assessment measures.

The California State Board of Education approved the charter for the school in February 1996, and the doors opened to students in September of that same year. Although it was a triumph for the community, that feeling of victory was soon overshadowed by the realities of opening and operating a school.

The many problems of a large urban school district, including lack of resources and the challenges of meeting day-to-day operations, found their way to the classrooms that had been founded with such high hopes and many prayers. It seemed to some that maybe the school would not be able to continue. But in February 2000, a new group of energetic and hopeful Indian community members volunteered to serve as board members. School year

2000–2001 proved to be a good one for students and staff. The subsequent positive changes culminated in a successful charter renewal for five years.

The story of the American Indian Charter School is a story of survival and belief that self-determination in education is the right of all Indian people. But it is a story made of real people who invested their careers and their lives, of people who trusted their children to the effort. Many people felt pain and frustration, and those who have been part of struggles to establish or keep things in communities know this well. Students and staff have come and remained, and it is they who understand the most about what they have—a small school with caring adults, a place where an Indian student can belong and have equal access to the gifts of education.

What will happen in the years to come? Like all stories, the outcome will depend on the actions of the people involved, and, most important, it will depend on the actions of the rest of the Indian community. The school will exist if the people want it and work for it, and if the people will honor those who have stepped forward to teach their children. The old values of honoring and respecting, of helping and working for the future, will need to be evidenced. Only then will the gains of the people not be lost and forgotten.

American Indian Preschool Graduation, 1974. *Top row, left to right:* Mark Abloogalook, Tonia Abloogalook, Jamie Nez, Mark Dixon, Sean Hata, Chris Bennett, —— Garcia. *Middle row:* Valerie Brown, Alice Brown, ——, Tray James, Melanie James, Bradley Ballenger, Marian Thomas, Earlene Drapeau. *Front row:* Tina Fourkiller, Crystal Abloogalook, Denise Ashenfelter, Toby James, ——.

Youth Empowerment
Program mural at
Intertribal Friendship
House, 8' X 15'.

I Am

I am a great granddaughter of the best basket weaver of the
    whole world.
I am the best friend of Gia because she's nice.
I am an Indian girl dancing at pow-wows.
I am a Pomo girl at ceremonies that are sad.
I am a person who loves her family so.
I am a person who loves horses because they gallop like the
    wind.
I am Ledah who loves her friends too much to talk about.

—Ledah Duncan, Pomo, Grade 4

"There are different spheres in the community. Then something
comes along that crosscuts those spheres and brings the community together. For years, that's what the preschool [later called
Hintil Kuu Ca] has done."
    —Wes Huss

The cover of the CD *WithOut Rezervation, Are You Ready for WOR?* says:

> From Oakland's mean streets come urban Native Americans rapping a politico-ethnic funk about the struggle of the red brother and red sister . . . so let the truth be told to young and old WithOut Rezervation.

Anaya's Song

Chris LaMarr
of WithOut Rezervation

(Anaya)
Anaya, I love my papa, I love my papa

(Chris)
What is it, what it means to be a pops
See she put me on top, responsibility don't stop
It never ends, it never will
And as long as I live girl, I'll be by your side for real
Not like the dad, I never had
Like a ghost some brothers are comatose
See they're, willing to step up to the plate with bat in hand
Yo MC, separate the child from man
We gotta learn to love our kids, yo
We gotta learn to love our kids,

(Anaya)
My name's Anaya
And I love my papa

(Chris)
A yo, plant the seed for the next generation
God is mine, he commanded your creation
A revelation and child we must learn
He chose you for the land and now it's your turn
I thank the stars and mother moon above
Yo, this is true love

What makes a man give up on his kid
Maybe you should live the life that I did
When you look in her eyes and see your own

Yeah, this papa's got it going on

What it is, what it means to be a pops
What it is, what it means to be a pops

To my loving daughter with all my heart
I wish upon you good times, a good life, a good start
I hope to teach you strength and pride
And as long as we're together everything will be all right
Now carry the torch pass from me to you
Take it to your child with peace to the old school
See I want the whole world to hear
I hope someday ya'll, ya'll can feed
You know I really love my kid
You know I really love my kid
I know you're young, your life just started
But you possess the cure for the broken heart
You filled my life with so much love, kid
I can't believe I live the life that I did
Now ready set, for hugs and kisses
Nothing in the world can make me miss this
Yo, real men take care of their own

What makes a man give up on his kid
Maybe you should live the life that I did
When you look in her eyes and see your own
Yeah, this papa's got it going on

What it is, what it means to be a pops
What it is, what it means to be a pops

Anaya's sunshine down on the best day
Cast your light through down come the purple rays
Baby, I'm amazed you came my way
And I think sometimes it's hard with child
Thinking back more hard times or more smiles
Must represent cuz our baby's heaven sent
Unmatched love there can be no regret
We gotta learn to love our kids, yo
We gotta learn to love our kids
See my little girl's next generation

Throw 'em up for WithOut Rezervation
Little kid represents our hopes, our dreams
Be a pops and you'll see what I mean
We gotta learn to live our kids
We gotta learn to live our kids

What makes a man give up on his kid
Maybe you should live the life that I did
When you look in her eyes and see your own
Yeah, this papa's got it going on

I love you, Papa
I love you, 'Naya

Percy with dog.

Been 49-ing

Author Unknown

Sweet on you, da one I want to kiss
every day and every night . . . wa ya hey, wa ya hey
You bring the stars and da moon in your eyes
every day and every night . . . wa ya hey, wa ya hey

The Cid

Julian Lang

Center of the World, Bad Moon, 1992

Note: A biased view exists. So we must first scuttle the idea that insinuates that the only valid indigenous cultural expression emanates from the remote Indian reservations, communities, and villages of this country. This being done, it is now possible to explore the subject "Indians living in the city" without feeling self-conscious.

Popular culture, media, and the American educational system itself have ingrained into us so many fallacies about Native cultures and Native Peoples that we should probably sue them. And perhaps we will. Today all of us have been miseducated to perceive Native Peoples and cultures as mere petrified remnants left over from the 1800s. The book you hold in your hands reveals a current experience that is both prevalent and long-lived: Native Peoples born and living in the cities of America.

Certain attitude adjustments are necessary to maneuver successfully through the four generations of history during which Native Peoples have been living in cities. The old urban American folkloric perception that people from the country are bumpkins and that city dwellers by nature are wiser, more worldly, and more sophisticated is reversed when the story is told in remote Native communities. Until recently, Native traditionalists, close to the land, noted that the sophisticated "sidewalk Indian," the city slicker, more often than not was ill-prepared to function in the traditional, spiritual, and natural worlds back home on the rez. In the last twenty years, the reversed bumpkin versus slicker condition has reversed again. A tide of urban Indian youth have been returning home to the rez specifically to learn and practice their traditional ways. Many urban Indians return home to the rez now for years at a time, "questing." Some return to the city (bringing their visions), some don't.

There is a view expressed by some of today's Native leaders that urban Indians are culturally and politically ludicrous somehow, that the urban Indian experience obstructs their connection with the land and their cultural beliefs and values. Yet some of the great accomplishments achieved by Native Peoples over the years were promoted by Indian people living in cities. Often urban Indians were the first to advocate to the non-Indian population the important political campaigns and calls for much needed positive change in Indian country. We need only recall the occupation of Alcatraz Island, the founding of D.-Q. University, Wounded Knee, and the Longest Walk. Each of these historic events and many more like them were strongly supported by Indian people and their friends living in cities. Ultimately the beneficiaries of this support and effort most often have been Indian people living back home on the rez.

In whatever way we might perceive the urban Indian, we can honestly say that Native Peoples have known cities for as long as they have existed on this land. We were living here long before they started spotting the hemisphere, for God's sake.

The city experience, like all life experiences, is as good as you make it. For most indigenous people or, better yet, for indigenous belief(s), the city is an abstraction: an ecobalanced reality gone unbelievably out of control. This is especially true for those who have never left their traditional worlds—that is, their aboriginal homelands. For many of them, the city is a place "outside." It's a part of the *other* Earth, the *other* way of life that exists beyond the boundary of their traditional homelands and outside the relationship many of them still maintain with the Earth.

I am of the Karuk People. We live in the remote mountains of northwestern California. Our word for *city* means "down below," usually referring to the San Francisco Bay Area. All during my childhood years, I remember the old people telling stories about those who lived "down below." As I have found, there is a long history binding my people to the Bay Area, along with many other California and non-California peoples.

There is a story about Captain John, a Hupa headman (one of our neighboring tribes), who was taken to San Francisco by the U.S. military during the late 1850s. The government's agents intended to prove to him just how futile it was for his people to continue fighting with the American soldiers. As the ship neared the Golden Gate, Captain John saw the city's first skyline. He asked his white escorts, "For how many generations has this town been here to be this big?" He was told that the San Francisco he was looking at was a mere ten years old.

Samfasiskûu (Karukacized English for San Francisco) has figured into some of the oldest Karuk songs, some of which are still sung today. For instance, there are a couple of men's love songs that tell how a sweetheart was taken away from home and carted away to Samfasiskûu. Rural California was one of the last holdouts refusing to institute Abe Lincoln's Emancipation Proclamation to abolish slavery in this country. Well into the 1870s, many young Indian women were kidnapped by white men under a legal pretext that they were available as indentured servants. The love songs of that era reveal the heartaches that the white man's strange law forced many of our men and women to endure. A dream song, composed a few years before the turn of the century, predicted the San Francisco earthquake of 1906. Clearly we have known San Francisco for a long time.

The subject of this book is Indians living in the city. I know the San Francisco Bay Area and have lived there. I continue to travel to these cities and others across the country in the course of my work. I have traveled throughout Indian country as well. Invariably I run into another Indian person who tells me something like, "I lived in Oakland for five years." Inevitably we discover that we know many of the same people. Then we're able to laugh about the same silly things because we know the same places and many of the same people. We call this "life in the Big Cid." Never mind that our discussion is taking place just below Black Butte on the San Ildefonso Pueblo in New Mexico. The same incident is as likely to happen when I meet a Seneca, Anishnabe, Dené, Puliklah, Tohono O'odham, Tongva, Lakota, Yaqui, or Tslagi in their own home country, thousands of miles from San Francisco.

In spite of the ongoing five-hundred-year-old political, social, economic, and spiritual campaigns against our ways of life, at least one member of every indigenous group that has survived the holocaust into the current year can be found in the city today. Recently I was in New York City and met one of the last remaining eighteen members of the people indigenous to Tierra del Fuego at the tip of South America. Native Hawaiian, Haida, Seminole, Micmac, you name it, one of their people lives in the city. There's a certain magical quality in knowing that so many tribal groups have persisted through the last decade of the twentieth century. And it's inspiring to meet someone from these nations.

If you know where Indian people congregate in the Bay Area, you can go there and find them: La Boheme Coffee Shop, where the AIMster artists hang; the Hilltop, where you're liable to see anyone; the Klub Kommotion, a performance space; the American Indian

Contemporary Arts Gallery; or the Intertribal Friendship House, the most long-lived community house for Native Peoples in the Bay Area. These are the obvious places to rub elbows with Indian people. There are many more. You never know who you might see at the International Indian Treaty Council offices (Rigoberta Menchú, for example), or at the News from Native California offices. I make it a habit to stop in to see Ruth Hopper at the UC Berkeley Native American studies office. I go to these places to hear what's really happening in the Cid. I'm both checking in *and* checking it out.

One of the beautiful things about Native life is that wherever we go, be it to the sacred High Country, down to the Mission District, over to the Fruitvale District, to the rez, or even to the beaches of Hawaii, we find our own people. And we're reminded that we share a history that has remained essentially positive and happy, in spite of often dire socioeconomic "things." Wherever we go, we are known by someone there. Wherever we go, we discover that we know someone there. The Ikxaréeyav, the Great Spirit, has created an interesting time for his people these days. He makes it possible for us to recognize, as if we could ever forget, that this land is *our* home, that we alone originate from this place.

It's true, you know, that enough can't be said about how destructive the city has been to Native Peoples over the generations. I, for one, however, have left behind many fond memories, friends, and loves in the city. And when I return there, I see the same beautiful smiles, and I get scolded for not writing or phoning more often. And I realize that going back to the city is a lot like returning home to the family.

May we all live to be a long time.

Blues-ing on the Brown Vibe

Esther G. Belin

I.

And Coyote struts down East 14th
feeling good
looking good
feeling the brown

melting into the brown that loiters .
rapping with the brown in front of the Native American Health
    Center
talking that talk
of relocation from tribal nation
of recent immigration to the place some call the United States
home to many dislocated funky brown

ironic immigration

more accurate tribal nation to tribal nation

and Coyote sprinkles corn pollen in the four directions
to thank the tribal people
        indigenous to what some call the state of California
        the city of Oakland
for allowing use of their land.

II.

And Coyote travels by Greyhound from Albuquerque, New Mexico,
    USA thru
Dinétah
to Oakland, California, USA
laughing
Interstate 40 is cluttered with RVs from as far away as Maine
traveling and traveling
to perpetuate the myth
Coyote kicks back for most of the ride
amused by the constant herd of tourists
amazed by the mythic Indian they create

at a pit stop in Winslow
Coyote trades a worn beaded cigarette lighter for roasted corn
from a middle-aged Navajo woman squatting
in front of a store

and Coyote squats alongside the woman
talking that talk
of bordertown blues
of reservation discrimination

blues-ing on the brown vibe
a bilagáana snaps a photo

the Navajo woman stands
holding out her hand
requesting some of her soul back
instead
she replaces her soul with a worn picture of George Washington on a
    dollar bill
and Coyote starts on another ear of corn
climbing onto the Greyhound
the woman
still squatting
waiting
tired of learning not to want
waits there for the return of all her pieces.

III.

And Coyote wanders
right into a Ponca sitting at the Fruitvale Bart station
next to the Ponca is a Seminole
Coyote struts up to the two
"Where ya' all from?"

the Ponca replies
"Oooklahooma"
pause
the Seminole silent watches a rush of people climb in and out of the
    train
headed for Fremont
the Seminole stretches his arms up and back still from the wooden
    benches
pause
he pushes his lips out toward the Ponca slowly gesturing that he too
    is from Oklahoma
Coyote wanders
"Where 'bouts?"

the Ponca replies
"Ponca City"
pause
the Seminole replies
"Seminole"

Coyote gestures to the Ponca
"You Ponca?"
the Ponca nods his head in affirmation
Coyote nods his head in content
to the Seminole
Coyote asks
"You Seminole?"
pause
the Seminole now watching some kids eating frozen fruit bars
nods his head

and Coyote shares his smokes with the two
and ten minutes later
they travel together on the Richmond train
headed for Wednesday night dinner at the Intertribal Friendship
    House

IV.

And Coyote blues-ing on the urban brown funk vibe
wanders
in and out of existence
tasting the brown
rusty at times
worn bitter from relocation.

"Our community is one family. We are interrelated and rely upon each family member to play a role in the community. We help others who are in need to ensure the ability of our community, our family, to remain strong and adapt to a continually changing environment. The Urban Indian Adult Education Program of United Indian Nations works to build community by reinforcing the ability of our family members to find within themselves the skills necessary to be self-sufficient. The survival of our community depends upon our traditional perspective [being] passed from generation to generation to help others in need. We are one family, one community."

   —*Sally Gallegos, Executive Director, United Indian Nations*

Indigenous People's Day

Saturday, October 10th, 1992 • **Martin Luther King, Jr. Park (Behind City Hall)** • **Berkeley** • **California**
To express appreciation for our survival and acknowledgement of our contribution to todays world community and in commemoration of our fallen patriots

Sunrise —Ceremony at the Berkeley waterfront
10:00 AM —Gather in the park
Noon —Dedication of Turtle Island Monument
2:00 PM —Motorcade leaves
2:00 to 4:00 —Procession to Shattuck Avenue

Berkeley Resistance 500 Task Force
Contact —(510) 548-1992
c/o Nancy Skinner
2180 Milvia — City Hall
Berkeley, California

— Purpose —
1. A commemoration of the now extinguished fires of native nations long gone and of the indigenous patriots and martyrs who stood for the values of indigenous people.
2. To acknowledge the contributions of indigenous peoples to todays modern society in arts, medicine, education, science, agriculture and government.
3. To affirm the survival and existence of tribal peoples all over the globe and to educate the public of the importance and symbiotic nature of our common destiny and that of the natural world.

GRAPHICS: Sal Garcia
CONCEPT: Zambrano-Garcia-Jennings

Sharing Our Colors

Tasina Ska Win (Lakota Harden—Minnecoujou/Yankton Lakota, HoChunk)

I was almost born in the Bay Area. Not too long before I was born, my mother Marilyn (Phillips) Harden was staying with my aunt Theodora, the mother of four boys, Russell, Dale, Bill, and Ted, helping to baby-sit when the twins (Bill and Ted) were babies. At that time, many members from both sides of my family were living in the Bay Area. Then during the 1960s, my mother's sister, Aunt Madonna Gilbert, moved to the Bay Area, and my brother and I came out to stay with her and my younger cousins in the Mission District. On my father's side, a few of my *dega*s lived in the area also. My aunt was involved in the takeover of Alcatraz Island, working on the school classes for the young children on the island. This and other instances led to continued organized resistance over the years. Our family was involved in the cofounding of the American Indian Movement (AIM), Women of All Red Nations (WARN), and the International Indian Treaty Council (IITC), and the "We Will Remember" Survival Group.

When I first got out of high school, I came back to Oakland to volunteer with the IITC, working on the newsletter and doing presentations and speaking engagements. This is how I started public speaking—representing the Treaty Council, AIM, WARN, and our "We Will Remember" Survival School in Porcupine, South Dakota. Then I moved permanently back to the Bay Area as an adult in 1987. I was thirty years old, with two children, seven and four years old. I went through quite a bit of "culture shock" coming from the Midwest, "cowboys and Indians" territory. I became involved with the Native students group at UC Berkeley, as well as with the pow-wow community of the region, the political community: the IITC, the Intertribal Friendship House, and the foremost spiritual community of Sundancers, attending sweats and ceremonies. It was great to meet so many Indians from all tribes. Part of me was grateful to find so many of my own; part of me was judgmental, for these "urban Indians" were so different from what I was familiar with, quite different, following some of the stereotypes that people thought of how an Indian was supposed to be.

For some of them who had grown up away from their people, it was all they knew.

One night I attended "The Revolutionary Nutcracker Sweetie," a dance theater production by the Dance Brigade, a multicultural women's dance troupe. (I later became a member and went on tour as part of the company, along with Gina Pacaldo [Apache/Chicana/Pilapina].) In this story, "there was a species of being who were beautiful, vibrant and thriving in their natural habitat . . . then men came to hunt and steal their colors . . . many of them were stripped bare and lost, and the others who survived hid deep and became cautious, mistrustful, even of their own who had lost their colors. . . . But eventually they would find each other, and they would once again survive and multiply by sharing their colors."

This story made me realize the many blessings I had received growing up in a traditional manner, and it was important for me to "share my colors." I learned quickly and realized that everyone is doing the best he or she can. I learned to celebrate our people wherever they are on their path. Learning to survive in the society AND maintain a traditional lifestyle is quite a balancing act, and I met many role models of Indians who learned to do this well, with the best intentions of maintaining our culture for the generations yet to come.

This also brought many of us into various arenas of the diverse Bay Area. I've learned so much and have been given such gifts from people of many "colors," many cultures, and many voices. As Indian people in a community of the Bay Area, we have brought our "contributions" to a thriving, growing, multicultural city, and we have thrived.

These contributions include films such as *Alcatraz Is Not an Island, Follow Me Home, The Way Home;* rap groups such as WithOut Rezervation and Culture of Rage; community projects and political struggles such as renaming Columbus Day as Indigenous People's Day and hosting Nelson Mandela when he visited the Bay Area; radio shows such as *Living on Indian Time;* art and cultural contributions to art galleries, to the Oakland Museum and the Yerba Buena Center for the Arts. All are ongoing expressions of our participation in the larger community around us. Through all these ways, we honor our ancestors and hope to clear new passages for our descendants yet to come.

No Longer Alone

Tasina Ska Win (Lakota Harden)

I have some friends who are Jews.
Who notice my respect for perpetual tradition, culture
understanding the importance of ritual.
AND we remember the fear of potential genocide at a
moments notice, that is centuries old.

I have some friends who are Japanese
who notice our kinship flowing, unending endurance
like the bamboo in the wind
AND we remember being torn from home
internment camps, reservations,
being seen as the bloodthirsty enemy.

I have some friends who are Black
Who notice we helped each other in the beginning to
survive, recognizing ancestors, our ways were the
same, connected to the mother
AND we remember we nurtured the generations even under
the taskmasters' whip.

I have some friends who are white
Who know the feeling of being orphaned, ancestry ripped
away, amalgamated in the vein of capitalism
AND we know the amnesia of isolation, disconnection
even from ourselves.

I have seen all your faces as you've entered my home,
Shared your pain, held up your hope
AND I notice and remember . . . we are no longer alone.

"They [Indian parents] talked about what had contributed to the decrease in the dropout rate and the other improvements in the educational opportunities and resources in the Bay Area over the last twenty years. Well, these changes are a result of lots of hard work by parents and staff. During this period of the late '70s there was fortunately a lot of funding, and we were able to build our educational programs. This grew directly out of the philosophy of the early parent group that felt the curriculum had to be culturally enriched within the school setting."

—Evelyn Lamenti, Director, Office of Indian Education, Oakland Public Schools

Preschoolers at play, 1974.

"The original idea had been to have a place to strengthen the young child, to give them a good positive image of themselves, an image of Indian people before they had to go into kindergarten in a mixed environment. We are helping support the families in giving the child self-confidence. Before, there wasn't even that option."

—Pat Bourgeois

"The education in the white world is for different purposes. There, one is successful as an individual through competition. In tribal society, what's important is finding one's place and relating to a large number of people. This is a very different perception of what a real human being is. The emphasis in public schools is on what can be measured, not how you feel about things, which can't be measured. Self-awareness and self-image is never tested in public schools."

—Wes Huss

"All the children are our children, and when one child suffers, that weakens the link for all of us. It is all of us that suffer. If we do something for that child, it is the community that is being strengthened."

—Ann Alton, Executive Director, Indigenous Nations Child and Family Agency

Thinking of home, 1974.

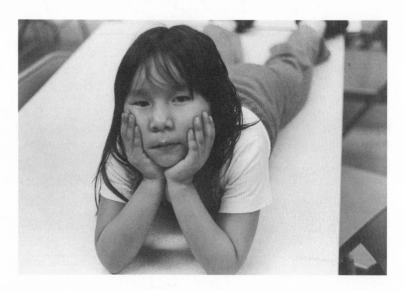

"At Hintil Kuu Ca, we try to instill pride in the students through knowing their tribe, their background, and their cultures, whether it is Native American or another culture, because we have many students of mixed cultures. We are a Native American diverse community. We try to teach to the whole child, and we let parents know that this is a safe place for them. Because we come from such a diverse community, we know that we can't do it alone, but have to have the support from the community as a whole. Really, we are the foundation for the children to get off to a good start in their education. For some of these children, we are the first contact they have had in the preschool with the educational system. And it's a good place to start."

    —Shirley Guevara, working with Hintil since 1984

"We were really blessed by the Elders in our families. We were given strong lectures on Indian ways from both sides. We always thought this was one of the reasons we stuck so close together all the time. We respect both of our families very much. We are loved by both sides, which is a good feeling. I think it has to come from the home from day one. We now have two grandchildren. They are Jemez, Navajo, Yurok, Pomo, and Wailaki."

    —Charlene and Joe Betsillie

"It has helped to have the grandparents involved. They taught the younger teachers to be more patient."

—*Pat Bourgeois*

At the American Indian Preschool, Hintil Kuu Ca, 1980. *Left to right:* Kevin Arnold, Marty Aranaydo, Gary Joe, Marla Want, Elmer St. John.

BIBLIOGRAPHIES

BIBLIOGRAPHY OF WORKS ON AMERICAN INDIANS IN THE BAY AREA

This bibliography is drawn from a more extensive one that Susan Lobo, Angelle Khachadoorian, Adrienne Brown, and Renee LaMarr compiled. A copy of the full bibliography may be obtained by contacting the Community History Project at Intertribal Friendship House, Oakland, California.

Ablon, Joan. 1964. "Relocated American Indians in the San Francisco Bay Area: Social Interaction and Indian Identity." *Human Organization* 23, no. 4: 296–304.

Alcatraz Revisited: The 25th Anniversary of the Occupation, 1969–1971. 1994. Special issue of *American Indian Culture and Research Journal* 18, no. 4. Articles by LaNada Boyer, Edward Castillo, Jack D. Forbes, Luis Kemnitzer, and Steve Talbot.

Antell, Judith. 1989. "American Indian Women Activists." Ph.D. diss., University of California, Berkeley.

Bean, Lowell, ed. 1994. *The Ohlone: Past and Present, Native Americans of the San Francisco Bay Region*. Menlo Park, Calif.: Ballena Press.

Blue Cloud, Peter. 1972. *Alcatraz Is Not an Island*. Berkeley, Calif.: Wingbow Press.

———. 1982. *Elderberry Flute Song: Contemporary Coyote Tales*. Trumansburg, N.Y.: Crossing Press.

Collier, John, Jr. 1981. *The People in Between: The Native American Past and Urban Assimilation*. Evanston, Ill.: Northwestern University.

Costo, Rupert. 1970. "Alcatraz." *The Indian Historian* (winter): 4–12.

Englander, Marilyn. 1985. "Through Their Words: Tradition and the Urban Indian Woman's Experience." Ph.D. diss., University of California, Santa Barbara.

Field, Les, Alan Leventhal, Dolores Sanchez, and Rosemary Cambra. 1992. *A Contemporary Ohlone Tribal Revitalization Movement: A Perspective from the Muwekma Costanoan/Ohlone Indians of the San Francisco Bay*. San Jose, Calif.: Muwekma Ohlone Indian Tribal Press.

Fortunate Eagle, Adam (a.k.a. Adam Nordwall). 1992. *Alcatraz! Alcatraz!: The Indian Occupation of 1969–1971*. Berkeley, Calif.: Heyday Books.

Garcia, Anthony Maes. 1988. "Home Is Not a House: Urban Relocation among American Indians." Ph.D. diss., University of California, Berkeley.

Graves, Theodore D. 1964. "Relocated American Indians in the San Francisco Bay Area." *Human Organization* 24: 296–304.

Hale, Janet Campbell. 1985. *The Jailing of Cecelia Capture.* Albuquerque: University of New Mexico Press.

Johnson, Troy R. 1996. *The Occupation of Alcatraz Island.* Urbana: University of Illinois Press.

Klein, D., E. Zahnd, B. Kolody, S. Holtby, and L. Midanik. 1995. *Final Report of the Pregnant and Parenting American Indian Study.* Berkeley, Calif.: Western Consortium for Public Health and San Diego State University Foundation. Submitted to California Department of Alcohol and Drug Programs.

Lobo, Susan. 1992. *American Indians in the San Francisco Bay Area and the 1990 Census.* Ethnographic report. Washington, D.C.: Center for Survey Methods Research, Bureau of the Census.

———. 2001. "Is Urban a Person or a Place? Characteristics of Urban Indian Country." In *American Indians and the Urban Experience,* edited by Susan Lobo and Kurt Peters. Walnut Creek, Calif.: AltaMira Press.

Mankiller, Wilma, and Michael Wallis. 1993. *Mankiller: A Chief and Her People.* New York: St. Martin's Press.

McDaniel, Mary. n.d. "My Grandmother Talked to the Water." In *I Am the Time of Fire,* edited by Jane Katz. New York: E. P. Dutton.

Means, Russell (with Marvin J. Smith). 1995. *Where White Men Fear to Tread: The Autobiography of Russell Means.* New York: St. Martin's Press.

Metcalf, Ann. 1982. "Navajo Women in the City: Lessons from a Quarter-Century of Relocation." *American Indian Quarterly* 6: 1–2.

Native American Research Group. 1975a. *American Indian Socialization to Urban Life: Final Report.* San Francisco: Institute for Scientific Analysis.

———. 1975b. *Native American Families in the City.* San Francisco: Institute for Scientific Analysis.

Ortiz, Simon. 1999. "The San Francisco Indians." In *Men on the Moon: Collected Short Stories by Simon Ortiz.* Tucson: University of Arizona Press.

Patterson, Vickie, and Susan Lobo. 1988. "Education: Oakland's Indian Education Programs, a Success Story." *News from Native California* 2, no. 4 (September–October): 23–24.

Smith, Paul Chaat, and Robert Allen Warrior. 1996. *Like a Hurricane: The Indian Movement from Alcatraz to Wounded Knee.* New York: New Press.

Willard, William. 1964a. *Navajo Urban Adjustment: Final Report to the National Institute of Mental Health.* San Francisco: Urban Indian Integration in the San Francisco Bay Area.

———. 1964b. *Pueblo Urban Adjustment: Final Report to the National Institute of Mental Health.* San Francisco: Urban Indian Integration in the San Francisco Bay Area.

BIBLIOGRAPHY ON URBANIZATION AND URBAN INDIAN COMMUNITIES

This short list of works that relate to urban Indian communities more broadly was excerpted from a larger bibliography that Susan Lobo, Renee LaMarr, Adrienne Brown, and Angelle Khachadoorian compiled. Contact the Community History Project at Intertribal Friendship House, Oakland, for the complete version. Those with a particular interest in relocation and relocation policy should take a look at Fixico's work cited here; for urban community descriptions, see in particular the Guillemin and Weibel-Orlando entries; and for broad-based writings on urban experiences, see Lobo and Peters.

Alexie, Sherman. 1996. *Indian Killer*. New York: Atlantic Monthly Press.

American Indian Policy Review Commission. 1976. *Report on Urban and Rural Non-Reservation Indians*. Final report to the American Indian Policy Review Commission. Washington, D.C.: U.S. Government Printing Office.

Baylor, Byrd. 1991. *Yes Is Better Than No*. Tucson, Ariz.: Treasure Chest.

Beck, David. 1988. *The Chicago American Indian Community 1893–1988: Annotated Bibliography and Guide to Sources in Chicago*. Chicago: NAES College Press.

Blackhawk, Ned. 1995. "I Can Carry on from Here: The Relocation of American Indians to Los Angeles." *Wacazo Sa Review* (fall): 16–29.

Deloria, Vine, Jr. 1970. "The Urban Scene and the American Indian." In *Indian Voices: The First Convocation of American Indian Scholars*. San Francisco: Indian Historian Press.

Fixico, Donald L. 1980. *Termination and Relocation: Federal Indian Policy, 1945–1960*. Albuquerque: University of New Mexico Press.

———. 2000. *Urban Indian Experience in America*. Albuquerque: University of New Mexico Press.

Guillemin, Jeanne. 1973. *Urban Renegades: The Cultural Strategy of American Indians*. New York: Columbia University Press.

Jackson, Deborah Davis. 2002. *Our Elders Lived It*. Dekalb: Northern Illinois University Press.

Joe, Jennie R., and Dorothy Lonewolf Miller. 1994. "Cultural Survival and Contemporary American Indian Women in the City." In *Women of Color in U.S. Society*, edited by M. B. Zinn and B. T. Dill. Philadelphia: Temple University Press.

Lobo, Susan, and Kurt Peters, eds. 1988. *American Indians and the Urban Experience*. Special issue of *American Indian Culture and Research Journal* 22, no. 4.

———, eds. 2001. *American Indians and the Urban Experience*. Walnut Creek,

Calif.: AltaMira Press. Includes chapters by Jack D. Forbes, Carol Miller, Octaviana Trujillo, Susan Lobo, Terry Straus, Debra Valentino, Joan Weibel-Orlando, Kurt Peters, Paivi Hoikkala, Julian Lang, David Beck, Angela Gonzales, Debrah Davis Jackson, Alex Julca, Darby Li Po Price, Renya Ramirez, Victoria Bomberry, and Christine Lowry.

Momaday, N. Scott. 1966. *House Made of Dawn*. New York: Harper Perennial.

NAES College Tribal Resource Center. 1994. *Urban Indian Bibliography* (annotated). Chicago: NAES College.

Nagel, Joane. 1996. *American Indian Ethnic Renewal, Red Power, and the Resurgence of Identity and Culture*. New York: Oxford University Press.

Sarris, Greg. 1994. *Grand Avenue*. New York: Hyperion.

———. 1998. *Watermelon Nights*. New York: Hyperion.

Silko, Leslie Marmon. 1986. *Ceremony*. New York: Penguin Books.

———. 1996. *Yellow Woman and a Beauty of the Spirit: Essays in Native American Life Today*. New York: Simon and Schuster.

Snipp, Mathew C. 1989. *American Indians: The First of the Land*. New York: Russell Sage Foundation.

Straus, Terry. 2000. *Native Chicago*. Chicago: University of Chicago Press.

Thornton, Russell. 1987. *American Indian Holocaust and Survival: A Population History Since 1492*. Norman: University of Oklahoma Press.

Thornton, Russell, Gary D. Sandefur, and Harold G. Grasmick. 1982. *The Urbanization of American Indians: A Critical Bibliography*. Bloomington: Newberry Library, Indiana University Press.

Vizenor, Gerald. 1990. *Crossbloods: Bone Courts, Bingo, and Other Reports*. Minneapolis: University of Minnesota Press.

Wadell, Jack O., and O. Michael Watson, eds. 1971. *The American Indian in Urban Society*. Boston: Little, Brown and Company.

Weibel-Orlando, Joan. 1991. *Indian Country, L.A.: Maintaining Ethnic Community in Complex Society*. Urbana: University of Illinois Press.

SOURCE ACKNOWLEDGMENTS

In-text quotations of individuals are from the Intertribal Friendship House Community History Project oral history archives unless noted below.

"Midnight," © Taweah Garcia, 1989, originally published in *The Memory Is Always in My Heart,* a collection of poetry from a workshop coordinated by Ramona Wilson. Reprinted with permission.

Excerpts from "Indian Life in the City: A Glimpse of the Urban Experience of Pomo Women in the 1930s," © Victoria D. Patterson. Originally published in *California History: The Magazine of the California Historical Society* 71, no. 3 (fall 1992). Reprinted with permission of the author.

"Euro-American Womanhood Ceremony," in *From the Belly of My Beauty,* by Esther G. Belin. Published by the University of Arizona Press, Tucson, 1999. Reprinted with permission of the author and publisher. Originally published in *Both Sides,* edited by David Fields (IAIA Press, 1994).

"Relocation: The Promise and the Lie," © Ray Moisa. An earlier version was published in *News from Native California* (May–June 1988). Reprinted with permission.

Quote by Irmlee Yellow Eagle from a brochure produced by the Intertribal Friendship House in the 1960s.

Quote by Glen Yellow Eagle from phone conversation with Susan Lobo, January 2001. Printed with permission.

"Quiet Desperation," song by Floyd Red Crow Westerman and Jimmy Curtiss. Lyrics © Floyd Red Crow Westerman. Reprinted with permission.

"A Winter Day," by George, Heather, Estella, and Manuel, originally published in *The Silver Moon Is Talking to the Stars,* a collection from a children's writing workshop coordinated by Ramona Wilson. Reprinted with permission.

"Goin' Back," lyrics and music © Floyd Red Crow Westerman, 1982.

"San Francisco," by Aggie Aranaydo; "I Am Indian," by Carlos Didrickson; "Skateboard," by Paul French; "My Father," by Tara Skidders; and "I Am," by Ledah Duncan, originally published in *Pretty Things Surround Me,* a collection from a children's writing workshop coordinated by Ramona Wilson. Reprinted with permission.

Sarah Poncho's fry bread recipe from a conversation with Susan Lobo, 2000. Published with permission.

Quotations of Rosalie McKay-Want from Judith Anne Antell, "American Indian Women Activists," Ph.D. dissertation, University of California, Berkeley, 1989.

Statements by Betty N. Cooper, Martin Waukazoo, and Evelyn Lamenti from an interview by Susan Lobo. Originally published in *Yacha* 1, no. 3 (1994).

"How Ruby Saves Laughter," in *From the Belly of My Beauty,* by Esther G. Belin. Published by the University of Arizona Press, Tucson, 1999. Reprinted with permission of the author and publisher. Originally in *Home Is in the Blood,* edited by Eddie Chucalate (IAIA Press, 1995).

"My Grandmother," by Martha Weaselbear; and "My Mom and Daddy," by Vickie Wilson, originally published in *A Mirror's Reflection,* a collection of poetry from a workshop coordinated by Ramona Wilson. Reprinted with permission.

"Anaya's Song," lyrics © Chris LaMarr, WithOut Rezervation, 1999.

"Been 49-ing." Author unknown.

"Blues-ing on the Brown Vibe," in *From the Belly of My Beauty,* by Esther G. Belin. Published by the University of Arizona Press, Tucson, 1999. Reprinted with permission of the author and publisher. Originally in *Neon Pow Wow: New Native American Voices of the Southwest,* edited by Anna Lee Walters (Northland Publishing, 1993).

Statement by Sally Gallegos, from "Urban Indian Adult Education Program" brochure, by Joyce McNair and Ashley Phillips.

Quotation of Charlene and Joe Betsillie. Originally published in *Yacha* 1, no. 2 (1994).

ILLUSTRATION CREDITS

Photographs, flyers, posters, calendars, and correspondence are from the Community History Project archives of the Intertribal Friendship House unless otherwise noted. Photographers, artists, and designers are credited below if information is available.

Published headlines are from a variety of newspapers, including the *Oakland Tribune, San Francisco Examiner, San Francisco News, Alameda Times Star, San Francisco Chronicle, Navajo Times,* and *Daily Californian.* Newspaper photographs are from the *Oakland Tribune, San Francisco News, Post-Enquirer,* and *Navajo News.*

ii–iii   "500 Years," © Paul Owns the Sabre, 1992.
xxiii   Editorial Committee, © Ken Tiger, 2001.

PART 1

xxiv, 16 Feast Day, Richmond Indian Village, 1954. Photographer unknown. Courtesy of Shirley Medina.
4   "Our Grandparents," Crow Children, 1910–1916. Photographer: Robert H. Lowie. Neg. 118816, courtesy of the American Museum of Natural History Library, New York.
4   "Our Children," Jenny and Toby James at the American Indian Preschool. Photographer: © Anthony M. Garcia, 1972.
5   "The Dancer." Artist: © Ed Willie.
13   Photographs from the *Oakland Tribune.*
15   Santa Fe Indian Village photographs. Photographer: Ruth Sarracino Hopper. Courtesy of Ruth Hopper family.
17   Feast Day, 1944, photographs and headlines from the *Post-Enquirer.*

PART 2

25   Headlines and photographs from the *San Francisco Examiner,* the *San Francisco News,* and the *Oakland Tribune.*
28   The Berryhill family, 1950s. Photographer unknown. Courtesy of Martha Berryhill.
31   Peggy Berryhill, 2000. Courtesy of Peggy Berryhill.
31   Untitled line drawing, man dreaming of the city. Artist: © Aaron Yava, 1975. Originally published in *Border Towns of the Navajo Nation* (Holmgangers Press, 1975). Reprinted with permission.

CONTRIBUTING EDITORS

Sharon Mitchell Bennett is Pomo Indian from Ukiah, California. She is a volunteer member of the advisory and editorial committees of the Community History Project at Intertribal Friendship House in Oakland. Sharon has been a resident of the Bay Area since the early 1960s. In addition, she joined the U.S. Navy and attended Merritt Community College and San Francisco State University to earn degrees in social work. She has worked for Intertribal Friendship House as its director and as a social worker for seventeen years. She has two great sons and two wonderful grandchildren.

Charlene Betsillie is a member of the Yurok tribe of northern California. In 1964, she came to the Bay Area on the Bureau of Indian Affairs Relocation Program. After arriving in the Bay Area, she learned about Intertribal Friendship House and volunteered and participated in many different programs there for many years. Since 1971 she has worked for California Indian Legal Services, a nonprofit legal services program that specializes in federal Indian law issues for Native California Indians and other Indian tribes. She was elected to the board of directors of Intertribal Friendship House and served as the chairperson for two years.

Joyce Keoke (White Flower Woman—Wahchaska Win) is Lakota and was born and raised in South Dakota. In the summer of 1955, when she was eighteen, she and her family left Standing Rock and came to Oakland through the relocation program. Although working at a number of jobs over the years, she was active in the Indian community, serving on the board of Intertribal Friendship House and on many committees for projects throughout the community. She also worked as the senior outreach coordinator at Intertribal Friendship House. She received training in museum curation from the Smithsonian Institution and was a research associate with the Community History Project for fourteen years, where she worked on this book. Joyce passed on to the spirit world in August 2000, leaving her service to the community as a legacy to three daughters and four grandchildren.

Geraldine Martinez Lira was born at home on the Rosebud Reservation in South Dakota, the youngest of eleven children. She attended both public and boarding schools. She married Martin Martinez and had eight children, among whom two are deceased. In 1956, she came to Oakland on relocation with her husband and three children. Four of their children were born in Oakland. Gerri became active in many spheres in the American Indian community upon her arrival in Oakland. She received her master's degree in social welfare in 1981 from San Francisco State University. Along with Marilyn St. Germaine and Susan Lobo, she founded the Community History Project in 1976 at Intertribal Friendship House. Although now retired, Gerri remains an active participant in the Bay Area American Indian community.

Susan Lobo was trained as a cultural anthropologist and now acts as a research, advocacy, and project design consultant primarily for American Indian tribes and community organizations in the United States and Central and South America. Since 1976 she has been the coordinator of the Community History Project at Intertribal Friendship House in Oakland and has taught at the University of California at Berkeley and at Davis, and at the University of Arizona. She has one daughter, Kelina. Her publications include *A House of My Own: Social Organization in the Squatter Settlements of Lima, Peru* (1982); *Native American Voices: A Reader* (2d ed., 2001); and *American Indians and the Urban Experience* (2001).

Marilyn LaPlante St. Germaine is an enrolled Blackfeet from Browning, Montana. She is the mother of five children, two now deceased, as well as the grandmother of nine and the great-grandmother of two. She came to Oakland on relocation with her family in September 1967. She received her master's degree in social welfare from San Francisco State University in 1981, while delivering social services to the American Indian population in Oakland, the East Bay, and surrounding areas. She continues this work today. In 1976, she cofounded the Community History Project at Intertribal Friendship House and has continued on the advisory board of the project to the present.